The IUL Edge

Build, Grow & Protect Tax-Free Wealth with Indexed Universal Life

Achieve Financial Security and Lasting Wealth with This One Little-Known 3-Letter Strategy

By: Stacie Gaston

The Table of The Content

Introduction_ Evolution and Tax Advantages of IUL

Indexed Universal Life (IUL) Insurance

Introduction and Core Features

Indexed Universal Life (IUL) insurance stands as a versatile financial instrument that has garnered significant attention for its unique ability to blend life insurance protection with the potential for cash value growth through equity market engagement. This chapter aims to provide a comprehensive overview of IUL insurance, meticulously delineating its primary features and setting it apart from other life insurance products like whole life and term life insurance.

At its core, an IUL policy offers a death benefit, which serves the traditional purpose of life insurance — providing financial security to beneficiaries following the policyholder's demise. However, it extends beyond mere coverage, incorporating an investment component that sets it apart in the realm of insurance products. This investment feature is what bestows IUL its distinct appeal and strategic advantage.

The mechanism of IUL revolves around its cash value accumulation linked inversely to the performance of a predetermined stock market index, commonly the S&P 500. It's crucial to understand that, while IUL policies allow for participation in stock market gains, they do so without direct investment in the stock market itself. Instead, the cash value portion of the premium payments accrues interest based, in part, on the upward movement of the index.

The hallmark feature that distinctly separates IUL from whole life and term life insurance is its flexibility. Unlike whole life insurance, which offers a fixed premium and guaranteed cash value growth, or term life insurance, which solely provides death benefits over a specified period without cash accumulation, IUL policies offer dynamic adaptability. Policyholders can adjust the face value of the policy and change premium payments within certain guidelines to tailor coverage to their evolving needs, making it an appealing choice for those seeking financial fluidity.

The cash value component of an IUL policy is particularly attractive due to its growth potential. While whole life policies provide predetermined interest returns, typically resulting in slower cash value accumulation, and term life policies offer no cash value at all, IUL's equity index-linked growth allows for potentially higher returns, subject to the performance of the chosen index. This feature provides policyholders with the opportunity to benefit from market upswings while simultaneously safeguarding against downturns through an inbuilt safety net — the policy's "floor" mechanism. This floor ensures that even if the index suffers a loss, the policy's cash value does not decrease, providing a significant edge in wealth preservation.

Moreover, IUL policies commonly cap the maximum interest that can be credited to the cash value in any given period. This cap limits the returns to a specific percentage, offering a balance between risk and reward. Even with a cap, the crediting potential often surpasses the fixed rate guarantee of traditional whole life insurance, thus providing a more enticing avenue for growth over time.

Importantly, an IUL policy affords tax-advantaged growth. The cash value accumulation within the policy grows on a tax-deferred basis, meaning that policyholders do not have to pay taxes on any growth until they decide to withdraw funds, if at all. This contrasts with investment vehicles like mutual funds or stocks, where dividends or capital gains are taxable when realized. Additionally, policyholders may leverage their cash value through tax-free policy loans or withdrawals, which can be strategically used to fund educational expenses, supplement retirement income, or finance other life goals.

To further highlight the distinctions, while both IUL and whole life insurance provide the benefit of lifetime coverage, IUL offers superior growth potential and flexible premium payments, features that whole life cannot emulate due to its rigid structure. In contrast, term life insurance, with its primary focus on providing temporary coverage, lacks any cash value component and thus does not serve as an investment instrument.

In summary, Indexed Universal Life insurance amalgamates the protective essence of life insurance with the dynamism of equity market participation. Through its structure, it offers policyholders an intricate yet robust avenue for protecting their legacy while concurrently building and preserving wealth. Its flexibility, potential for cash value growth, and tax-advantaged nature render it a compelling choice for individuals across various stages of life who aspire to achieve comprehensive financial security with growth potential. Understanding and leveraging these attributes can empower policyholders to meet financial objectives with a nuanced, sophisticated approach to life insurance.

Core Benefits of IUL

Indexed Universal Life (IUL) insurance has emerged as a compelling financial instrument for those seeking a versatile combination of protection and growth potential. Its allure can be attributed to several core benefits that cater to the modern policyholder's diverse financial needs. Let us delve into these benefits, focusing on the flexibility, security, and growth potential that make IUL insurance indispensable.

Flexibility in Premium Payments

One of the most attractive features of IUL insurance is its flexibility in premium payments. Unlike traditional insurance products that require fixed regular premiums, IUL policies allow policyholders to adjust their premiums according to their financial situation. This accommodates individuals who may experience fluctuating incomes, such as business owners or freelancers. Policyholders can choose to pay the minimum required premium to keep the policy active or increase their payments to enhance the cash value accumulation. This adjustability means that the policy can be tailored to meet your financial goals throughout different life stages.

Death Benefits with Financial Protection

At its core, life insurance provides financial security to your beneficiaries. With IUL, the death benefit is not just a static figure but a dynamic component that can be adjusted to meet your evolving needs. Policyholders can choose between a level death benefit, which remains constant, or an increasing death benefit, where the payout can grow as the cash value within the policy appreciates. This offers not only financial protection to loved ones in the event of the policyholder's death but also ensures that, as personal circumstances change, the policy can adapt in response.

Growth Potential through Cash Value Accumulation

The growth of cash value is arguably one of the most distinctive features of an Indexed Universal Life policy. Unlike whole life insurance, where the growth rate is fixed, or variable life insurance, which carries investment risk, IUL products are tied to the performance of stock market indices, like the S&P 500. This index-linked approach offers policyholders the opportunity to benefit from market upswings while simultaneously being shielded from market downturns. Most IUL policies come with a cap and a floor, meaning that while there are limits on the maximum growth during bull markets, there is also a safeguard against losses in bear markets. This ensures that your cash value can grow over time in a risk-managed environment.

Diverse Allocation Options

IUL policies offer a variety of allocation options tailored to different risk appetites and financial objectives. Policyholders can choose how their cash value is credited based on the performance of one or several indices. This allocation is flexible and can be adjusted, allowing policyholders to respond to market changes or personal investment preferences. This means you're not locked into a single strategy and can pivot as your financial goals or market conditions change.

Tax Advantages

Another pivotal advantage of IUL insurance is its compelling tax benefits. The cash value grows on a tax-deferred basis, allowing policyholders to compound their wealth without the drag of annual taxes. Furthermore, the death benefit is generally received income-tax-free by beneficiaries, providing substantial savings and maximizing the financial legacy left behind. Additionally, through strategic policy loans and withdrawals, policyholders can access the accumulated cash value in a tax-advantaged manner, leveraging their policy as a potential source of tax-free retirement income.

Legacy and Estate Planning

Beyond personal financial security, IUL insurance plays a strategic role in legacy and estate planning. The combination of death benefit and cash value growth forms a potent tool in ensuring that wealth is efficiently transferred to beneficiaries. It can serve as a mechanism to address estate taxes or equalize inheritance among heirs, providing control over how wealth is distributed and utilized by future generations.

Conclusion of Benefits

The manifold benefits of IUL insurance make it an exceptional choice for individuals looking to amalgamate financial protection with growth potential. Its inherent flexibility in premium payments and benefit structuring enables policyholders to tailor their coverage to meet personal life circumstances. The growth opportunity through cash value, powered by index-linked strategies, introduces a level of dynamism that traditional whole life or universal life products may lack. Additionally, the tax advantages further bolster its utility as a robust financial planning tool that transcends mere insurance. As such, Indexed Universal Life insurance stands as a multidimensional product designed to secure and enhance the financial well-being of policyholders and their beneficiaries alike.

Historical Development and Evolution of IUL

The Historical Development and Evolution of Indexed Universal Life (IUL) insurance is a fascinating journey that reflects the broader changes and innovations within the financial services industry. To fully appreciate the current versatility and appeal of IUL, it's essential to explore its origins and the various evolutionary milestones that have shaped it into a powerful financial instrument.

In the beginning, life insurance was primarily dominated by traditional whole life policies, which offered guaranteed premiums, death benefits, and a modest cash value accumulation. While these policies provided security and certainty, they lacked flexibility and the potential for significant cash value growth. This limitation sparked the need for innovative solutions that could blend the benefits of life insurance with opportunities for investment growth.

The seeds for what would eventually become Indexed Universal Life insurance were planted in the 1970s and 1980s with the introduction of Universal Life (UL) insurance. UL revolutionized the insurance landscape by introducing flexibility in premium payments and death benefits. Policyholders could adjust their premiums and coverage amounts to better align with their changing financial circumstances.

Importantly, UL also permitted the cash value component of the policy to earn interest at rates tied to the insurer's portfolio performance, offering greater growth potential than traditional whole life insurance.

While UL provided much-needed flexibility and a degree of cash value growth, it soon became clear that tying cash value interest rates solely to the insurer's portfolio had its limitations, especially during periods of fluctuating interest rates. Consumers were becoming increasingly sophisticated and sought greater growth opportunities without the direct exposure to risk associated with the burgeoning variable life insurance products that directly linked cash value growth to market performance.

This consumer demand for a sweet spot between conservative UL and the more aggressive variable life insurance led to the creation of Indexed Universal Life insurance in the late 1990s. The primary innovation of IUL was its unique crediting strategy: instead of linking the cash value to the insurer's general portfolio or directly to a stock market index, IUL policies allowed policyholders to earn interest based on the performance of a market index, such as the S&P 500, while providing downside protection through minimum guaranteed interest rates.

The introduction of indexed crediting was transformative. It addressed the dual consumer desires for growth potential and safety. Policyholders could benefit from the upward movements of a stock index without the risk of losing the principal during market downturns. This capacity for growth, combined with the tax-advantaged nature of life insurance, made IUL an attractive choice for those seeking to balance risk and reward.

As the 21st century progressed, IUL continued to evolve with further enhancements to meet changing market conditions and consumer preferences. For instance, insurers began offering a wider range of index choices, including international and sector-specific indices, giving policyholders more options to tailor their growth strategies. Furthermore, the introduction of vol-control indices aimed to reduce volatility while providing stable returns, appealing to risk-averse investors.

The adaptability of IUL has also been evident in its response to economic and legislative changes. As regulators imposed stricter guidelines post the 2008 financial crisis, IUL policies were structured to assure compliance while delivering superior performance in a low-interest-rate environment. Additionally, innovations such as hybrid policies that combine long-term care benefits with life insurance have further cemented IUL's place as a multifaceted financial solution.

The resilience of IUL is not merely a reflection of its structural and strategic enhancements but also a testament to its enduring appeal. As financial technology advances, IUL continues to integrate digital tools to enhance customer experience and policy management. Easy access to policy information, online premium adjustments, and accelerated underwriting through data analytics are just some of the technological evolution landmarks that continue to keep IUL relevant and desirable.

In essence, the historical development of Indexed Universal Life insurance is a story of continuous growth, strategic innovation, and responsiveness to the needs of consumers and the market. From its roots in Universal Life to its current iteration as a flexible, growth-oriented, and tax-efficient financial tool, IUL has cemented itself as a lasting and evolving pillar in the landscape of life insurance and broader financial planning. This adaptability not only underscores the resilience of IUL but also highlights its forward-looking potential as a wealth-building strategy in an ever-changing financial world.

Tax Advantages of IUL in Detail

Indexed Universal Life (IUL) insurance presents a compelling and versatile option when viewed through the lens of tax-efficiency—especially when compared to traditional financial vehicles such as 401(k)s, IRAs, and mutual funds. As a hybrid financial tool, IUL not only provides essential life insurance coverage, but it also enables policyholders to capitalize on powerful tax advantages that can significantly enhance long-term wealth accumulation and legacy planning.

To truly appreciate the tax benefits that IULs offer, it's beneficial to explore their characteristics alongside those of other financial instruments. Let's delve into how IULs stand out in three fundamental areas: tax-deferred growth of cash value, tax-free loans and withdrawals, and tax-free death benefits.

1. Tax-Deferred Growth

In IULs, the cash value component grows on a tax-deferred basis. This means that any earnings from the policy's underlying investments, typically linked to a stock market index like the S&P 500, do not incur taxes until you decide to withdraw them. This mirrors the tax advantages seen in 401(k) and traditional IRA accounts, allowing for compounding without immediate tax consequences, which can dramatically accelerate accumulation over the years. Meanwhile, mutual funds, particularly those held outside of tax-advantaged accounts, generate taxable events with each distribution or sale. Investors are liable for taxes on dividends and capital gains annually, which can stymie growth potential. IULs, thus, provide a similar tax shield found in retirement accounts while potentially offering higher returns linked to market performance without the taxation hurdles faced by mutual funds.

2. Tax-Free Loans and Withdrawals

One of the most enticing features of an IUL policy is the ability to access its cash value tax-free through policy loans and strategic withdrawals. This is distinct from traditional retirement accounts like 401(k)s and IRAs, where withdrawals are generally subject to ordinary income tax, and early withdrawals incur additional penalties unless specific conditions are met. With an IUL, policyholders can borrow against their accumulated cash value without triggering a taxable event, as these loans are considered non-taxable. As long as the policy remains active and the withdrawals don't exceed the cost basis, the withdrawals can also be tax-free. This sets a unique precedent for accessing funds during a policyholder's lifetime, offering unparalleled flexibility to finance major life expenses like college tuition, mortgages, or medical expenses without worrying about immediate tax implications.

3. Tax-Free Death Benefit

IUL policies also stand out with their tax-free death benefits, granted to beneficiaries upon the policyholder's demise. This provides a significant estate planning advantage when contrasted with the tax implications associated with the transfer of traditional taxable investment accounts. In a world where estate taxes can erode a significant portion of the inheritance, IULs provide a means to preserve capital across generations. While tax-deferred vehicles like traditional IRAs or 401(k)s do provide their versions of inheritance benefits, they are often subject to compulsory distribution rules, potentially resulting in hefty tax bills for heirs. The death benefit of an IUL, in contrast, reinforces its mission as a tool for wealth preservation and transfer, seamlessly bridging wealth to future generations without the associated burden of taxation.

IULs, therefore, offer a rare trifecta of tax benefits: tax-deferred growth, tax-free loans and withdrawals, and tax-free death benefits. When situated in juxtaposition with other financial mechanisms, it becomes apparent that IULs possess a unique versatility and efficacy that can be leveraged for both growth and protection. Its design affords policyholders the nimbleness to navigate financial objectives while strategically managing tax liabilities.

In conclusion, as financial landscapes become increasingly complex and punitive with respect to taxation, the Indexed Universal Life insurance product emerges as a potent strategy to surmount future economic challenges. By understanding and utilizing the nuanced tax advantages provided by IULs, policyholders can create a financial strategy that aligns with both wealth-building aspirations and preservation mandates. The knowledge and application of these principles can empower individuals to optimally position themselves within the broader theme of tax-efficient financial planning, ensuring that every component of their financial ecosystem works toward the ultimate goal of sustained and secured wealth.

Common Misconceptions and Challenges with IUL

Indexed Universal Life (IUL) insurance is a dynamic financial tool often misunderstood due to its complexity and market-based components. As we delve into this chapter, we will illuminate common misconceptions surrounding IUL, addressing concerns related to cost, complexity, and the inherent risks of linking life insurance with financial markets. We will also navigate potential downsides while demonstrating strategies to mitigate them through judicious planning and adept policy design.

Misconception 1: IUL is Too Costly

A prevalent misconception is that IUL policies are prohibitively expensive. It's essential to recognize that while the cost of IUL policies might be higher than for term insurance, they offer different value propositions. IUL combines the protective features of life insurance with the cash accumulation potential of equity market-linked returns. Unlike term insurance, which provides only a death benefit, IUL seeks to create a living benefit through cash value accumulation, something akin to having a safety net with a built-in savings component.

Costs in an IUL policy can arise from insurance charges, administrative fees, and the cost of the riders attached to the policy. However, these costs can be strategically managed with thoughtful design. For instance, policyholders can tailor their policies to align with their financial objectives and constraints, ensuring that premium payments and policy terms are appropriate for their circumstances. By leveraging flexible premium payments and adjustments over time, policyholders can manage costs more effectively, aligning them with their changing life situations and goals.

Misconception 2: IUL is Overly Complex

Another frequently cited concern is the perceived complexity of IUL policies. Prospective policyholders might feel overwhelmed by the myriads of options, riders, and terms associated with IUL. While it is true that IUL products offer a high degree of flexibility and numerous options for customization, this complexity can be demystified with adequate education and financial advice.

An understanding of the core elements of an IUL policy—such as the death benefit, cash value accumulation, and the indexing mechanism— can significantly enhance a policyholder's ability to make informed decisions. Financial advisors play a pivotal role in this educational process, guiding clients through the intricacies of policy features and helping tailor them to meet specific financial goals. By breaking down the policy's components and functions, advisors can help dispel the myth of complexity, empowering clients to take advantage of the product's flexibility.

Misconception 3: Market Index Risk

Concerns about risk often center on the linking of IUL policies to market indices, such as the S&P 500. There's a notion that this linkage introduces a level of volatility and risk equivalent to investing directly in the stock market. However, this is a misunderstanding of how IUL policies operate.

In reality, IUL policies are designed to offer upside potential tied to the performance of a market index while protecting the policyholder against downside risk. This is achieved through a feature commonly known as the "floor," which ensures that the cash value will not decline due to negative index performance; typically, this floor is set at 0%. As a result, while the policy benefits from positive market performance, it avoids losses during market downturns. This risk-reward balance makes IUL a compelling choice for those seeking growth without exposing their capital to direct market risks.

Potential Downsides and Mitigation Strategies

While IUL offers significant advantages, it also comes with potential downsides that necessitate careful consideration. One such downside is the interest rate cap that insurers may impose, limiting the growth of cash value in times of strong market performance. Policyholders should understand these caps and work closely with financial advisors to set realistic expectations for growth.

A lapse in the policy is another risk if premiums are not adequately maintained. To mitigate this, it's crucial to establish a robust premium payment strategy and regularly review the policy performance against original expectations and market conditions. Regular policy reviews ensure that adjustments can be made in response to both personal and economic changes, maintaining the policy's alignment with intended goals.

Lastly, the prolonged commitment required by IUL policies can be daunting. Policyholders should enter into an IUL agreement with a clear long-term strategy in mind, supported by thorough financial planning. This foresight enables them to weather economic fluctuations and personal financial challenges.

In conclusion, while IUL policies can be subject to misconceptions and challenges, understanding and educating oneself about these aspects is crucial. Through informed decision-making and strategic planning, policyholders can harness the benefits of IUL, creating a robust, flexible financial tool that not only offers life insurance protection but also facilitates tax-advantaged wealth-building.

The Ideal Candidate for IUL

In the realm of financial planning, the Indexed Universal Life (IUL) insurance policy emerges not as a one-size-fits-all solution but as a strategic instrument tailored for a discerning set of individuals. Understanding the ideal candidate for IUL investment involves examining a blend of financial goals, risk tolerance, and life stage. By carefully analyzing these factors, one can identify those who stand to benefit most from incorporating this versatile tool into their wealth-building strategy.

Firstly, let us consider financial goals, the compass directing one's investment journey. The ideal IUL candidate is someone with clearly defined objectives that align with both wealth accumulation and legacy building. Those who value both a tax-deferred growth mechanism and a tax-free distribution opportunity will find IUL particularly appealing. It allows policyholders to build cash value over time, which can then be leveraged for significant life events such as retirement, funding higher education for children, or establishing a philanthropic legacy. Individuals seeking to diversify their strategies beyond traditional tax-qualified plans like IRAs and 401(k)s will find that IUL policies complement these vehicles with their unique, tax-advantaged benefits.

Next, examine risk tolerance, the measure of an individual's comfort with investment variability. IUL policies cater to those with a moderate risk appetite; they cater to those looking to capture the upside potential of market-linked returns without direct exposure to market downturns. Unlike investing directly in equities, which subjects capital to potential loss during market dips, IULs offer a safety net with a guaranteed minimum interest credit. This appeal is particularly potent for individuals seeking growth opportunities tied to equity indexes like the S&P 500, while still enjoying the peace of mind that comes from knowing their principal is protected.

Also critical is the stage of life at which a potential policyholder might find themselves. IUL is most advantageous for individuals in the wealth accumulation phase, typically those in their 30s to 50s, who have established income streams and seek to enhance their retirement portfolios. Younger investors, while still benefiting from the long-term growth potential of IUL, may not see the immediate advantages due to the initial higher funding requirements, which could be challenging without a considerable disposable income.

Moreover, those who are in peak earning years or high tax brackets will particularly appreciate the tax deferment on cash value accumulation and the tax-free policy loans and withdrawals IULs offer. As these individuals start considering retirement options, IUL policies can act as a supplementary income stream, providing liquidity and flexibility. For the astute business owner or professional, an IUL serves as both a personal financial asset and a tool for business succession planning or executive compensation arrangements, thanks to its tax advantages and potential for significant cash value growth.

Equally important is evaluating one's future insurability. Individuals who foresee a decline in health but are currently insurable should seriously consider initiating an IUL policy while rates and conditions are favorable. This forethought secures life insurance coverage along with the added financial benefits, regardless of future health changes.

Moreover, individuals with dependents, such as children or non-working spouses, often prioritize securing a financial safety net, which further highlights the attractiveness of IUL's death benefit. This benefit offers peace of mind, ensuring family members have financial protection in the policyholder's absence, making it a cornerstone of long-term family financial planning.

In summary, the quintessential IUL client is a financially astute individual with a vision for both immediate and future financial goals. They exhibit a balanced risk tolerance, appreciate the nuances of tax efficiency, and are typically in a life stage where long-term growth, income supplementation, and wealth transfer are priorities. By aligning IUL with their comprehensive financial strategy, they can effectively harness its benefits to construct a robust economic future, characterized by growth, protection, and legacy. This strategic alignment makes IUL an investment choice and a pivotal element in a thoughtfully curated financial portfolio.

Chapter 1_Understanding Indexed Universal Life (IUL) Insurance

Defining Indexed Universal Life (IUL) Insurance

Indexed Universal Life (IUL) insurance stands as a versatile financial instrument that has garnered significant attention for its unique ability to blend life insurance protection with the potential for cash value growth through equity market engagement. This chapter aims to provide a comprehensive overview of IUL insurance, meticulously delineating its primary features and setting it apart from other life insurance products like whole life and term life insurance.

At its core, an IUL policy offers a death benefit, which serves the traditional purpose of life insurance providing financial security to beneficiaries following the policyholder's demise. However, it extends beyond mere coverage, incorporating an investment component that sets it apart in the realm of insurance products. This investment feature is what bestows IUL its distinct appeal and strategic advantage.

The mechanism of IUL revolves around its cash value accumulation linked inversely to the performance of a predetermined stock market index, commonly the S&P 500. It's crucial to understand that, while IUL policies allow for participation in stock market gains, they do so without direct investment in the stock market itself. Instead, the cash value portion of the premium payments accrues interest based, in part, on the upward movement of the index.

The hallmark feature that distinctly separates IUL from whole life and term life insurance is its flexibility. Unlike whole life insurance, which offers a fixed premium and guaranteed cash value growth, or term life insurance, which solely provides death benefits over a specified period without cash accumulation, IUL policies offer dynamic adaptability. Policyholders can adjust the face value of the policy and change premium payments within certain guidelines to tailor coverage to their evolving needs, making it an appealing choice for those seeking financial fluidity.

The cash value component of an IUL policy is particularly attractive due to its growth potential. While whole life policies provide predetermined interest returns, typically resulting in slower cash value accumulation, and term life policies offer no cash value at all, IUL's equity index-linked growth allows for potentially higher returns, subject to the performance of the chosen index. This feature provides policyholders with the opportunity to benefit from market upswings while simultaneously safeguarding against downturns through an inbuilt safety net the policy's "floor" mechanism. This floor ensures that even if the index suffers a loss, the policy's cash value does not decrease, providing a significant edge in wealth preservation.

Moreover, IUL policies commonly cap the maximum interest that can be credited to the cash value in any given period. This cap limits the returns to a specific percentage, offering a balance between risk and reward. Even with a cap, the crediting potential often surpasses the fixed rate guarantee of traditional whole life insurance, thus providing a more enticing avenue for growth over time.

Importantly, an IUL policy affords tax-advantaged growth. The cash value accumulation within the policy grows on a tax-deferred basis, meaning that policyholders do not have to pay taxes on any growth until they decide to withdraw funds, if at all. This contrasts with investment vehicles like mutual funds or stocks, where dividends or capital gains are taxable when realized. Additionally, policyholders may leverage their cash value through tax-free policy loans or withdrawals, which can be strategically used to fund educational expenses, supplement retirement income, or finance other life goals.

To further highlight the distinctions, while both IUL and whole life insurance provide the benefit of lifetime coverage, IUL offers superior growth potential and flexible premium payments, features that whole life cannot emulate due to its rigid structure. In contrast, term life insurance, with its primary focus on providing temporary coverage, lacks any cash value component and thus does not serve as an investment instrument.

In summary, Indexed Universal Life insurance amalgamates the protective essence of life insurance with the dynamism of equity market participation. Through its structure, it offers policyholders an intricate yet robust avenue for protecting their legacy while concurrently building and preserving wealth. Its flexibility, potential for cash value growth, and tax-advantaged nature render it a compelling choice for individuals across various stages of life who aspire to achieve comprehensive financial security with growth potential. Understanding and leveraging these attributes can empower policyholders to meet financial objectives with a nuanced, sophisticated approach to life insurance.

Indexed Universal Life (IUL) insurance has emerged as a compelling financial instrument for those seeking a versatile combination of protection and growth potential. Its allure can be attributed to several core benefits that cater to the modern policyholder's diverse financial needs. Let us delve into these benefits, focusing on the flexibility, security, and growth potential that make IUL insurance indispensable.

Comprehensive Overview of IUL Benefits

Flexibility and Adjustability

One of the hallmark benefits of Indexed Universal Life insurance is its inherent flexibility. Policyholders can adjust their premium payments and death benefits, which is a significant departure from the rigid structures of whole life or term insurance. This flexibility allows individuals to tailor their policies to adapt to changing financial circumstances over the course of their lives. For instance, during high-earning periods, one might choose to increase premium payments to build cash value, while during leaner times, payments can be minimized while still maintaining the policy.

Participation in Market Gains

At the core of an IUL policy is the ability to benefit from the upward movements of market indexes, such as the S&P 500, without directly investing in them. This feature is particularly attractive as it offers the potential for higher cash value accumulation compared to traditional fixed-rate policies. By linking the growth of the policy's cash value to a market index, policyholders can enjoy the fruits of a bullish market while having the peace of mind that comes with knowing they are not directly exposed to market volatility.

Downside Protection

While IUL policies offer the chance to tap into market gains, they also provide a crucial safety net: downside protection. IUL policies typically include a guarantee that ensures policyholders will not lose their initial investment due to market downturns. This safety feature, often referred to as a "floor," means that even in years when the stock market underperforms, the cash value of the policy remains protected from loss. This offers a powerful blend of opportunity and security, allowing policyholders to sleep soundly, knowing their financial future is safeguarded against market unpredictability.

Tax-Advantaged Growth

Tax efficiency is one of the most compelling benefits of Indexed Universal Life insurance. The cash value grows tax-deferred, much like in Roth IRA, meaning policyholders do not pay taxes on the accumulated growth unless they withdraw more than the premiums paid. Furthermore, the potential exists to access the cash value in the form of policy loans or withdrawals without triggering taxes, provided that the policy is structured and managed properly. This feature makes IUL an attractive option for individuals looking to supplement retirement income or tackle significant financial goals while minimizing tax liabilities.

Death Benefit and Living Benefits

The primary purpose of any life insurance policy is to provide a death benefit to beneficiaries. An IUL policy maintains this fundamental role, ensuring financial protection for the insured's family in the event of their passing. However, modern IUL policies often come with additional living benefits that can be exceedingly beneficial. For instance, some policies include riders for long-term care or critical illness, allowing policyholders to access part of their death benefit in the event of qualifying medical conditions. This dual utility enhances the value proposition of IUL, making it not just a death benefit tool, but a comprehensive life management solution.

Estate Planning and Legacy Building

For those focused on estate planning, an IUL policy offers unique advantages. The death benefit from a life insurance policy, including IUL, is typically tax-free for beneficiaries. This ability to pass on wealth without the encumbrance of taxes makes IUL a strategic component in legacy planning, allowing policyholders to maximize the benefits passed on to future generations. Additionally, with careful planning, IUL policies can be used to fund trusts or as part of charitable giving strategies, aligning with broader personal or philanthropic goals.

Protection Against Inflation

Lastly, the connection of an IUL policy's cash value to market indexes provides a natural hedge against inflation. As the value of money erodes over time due to inflation, the growth potential tied to market performance allows the cash value to keep pace with or exceed inflation rates. This ensures that the policy's benefits hold their purchasing power over the years, providing more substantial and meaningful financial security for the policyholder and their beneficiaries.

In summary, Indexed Universal Life insurance is a multifaceted financial tool that delivers a compelling array of benefits. From flexible premium and benefit adjustments to tax advantages and inflation protection, the IUL stands out as a versatile instrument in financial planning. Its blend of insurance and investment features makes it an attractive proposition for individuals looking to secure their financial future while enjoying the potential for growth and providing a legacy for their heirs.

The Evolution of IUL as a Financial Tool

The journey of Indexed Universal Life (IUL) insurance is one marked by innovation, adaptation, and a keen understanding of consumers' financial needs. To fully appreciate its evolution as a financial tool, it's essential to explore the confluence of circumstances that birthed IUL policies and transformed them into the robust financial instruments they are today.

In the latter half of the 20th century, life insurance witnessed significant changes. Term life insurance, with its simple, straightforward offering, remained a cornerstone for providing protection. However, the growing need for policies that could offer not merely a death benefit but also a mechanism for savings catalyzed the creation of universal life insurance in the 1980s. Universal Life (UL) insurance offered flexibility in premium payments and death benefits, and it allowed policyholders to accumulate a cash value component.

UL insurance was only the first step. Policyholders began to demand more, particularly an opportunity to link their cash value growth directly to the market's potential upside, without direct exposure to its downsides. This demand coincided with the era's bull markets and the growing awareness of the importance of diversifying one's financial portfolio. Enter Indexed Universal Life insurance, a product that debuted in the late

1990s, combining the benefits of both market-linked growth potential and the protection of a traditional insurance policy.

The core innovation of IULs lies in how they credit interest to the policy's cash value. The cash value growth is tied to the performance of a specific financial index, commonly the S&P 500, giving the policyholder a chance to benefit from market uptrends. However, unlike direct market investments, IUL policies include a safeguard—typically a 0% floor—that ensures if the index performs negatively, the policyholder's principal is not at risk. This element of downside protection makes IULs attractive to risk-averse investors as well as those looking to ensure their financial strategies include built-in safety nets.

As market conditions and personal wealth-building philosophies continued to evolve, so too did the structure of IULs. Insurance companies began competing to offer the most innovative policy designs and features—such as increasingly competitive participation rates, interest bonuses, and the introduction of various market index options beyond the ubiquitous S&P 500. The flexibility of IULs allows policyholders to adjust their death benefits, alter premium payment schedules, and utilize policy loans—all features that align well with a modern lifestyle that values adaptability and control.

The maturation of IUL as a financial tool was also fueled by changing tax environments. As governments continuously adjust tax laws, products like IUL insurance that offer tax-deferred cash value growth and tax-free loans became even more appealing. These features cater to individuals seeking not only wealth protection but also effective strategies for reducing tax liability. The ability to withdraw funds or take policy loans tax-free provides policyholders with a financial cushion for emergencies, retirement income supplements, or funding significant life events without the looming specter of tax implications.

Technological advancement played its own part in the evolution of IUL. The sophistication of digital platforms allowed for more precise tracking of cash values and index performance, leading to an era where policyholders could have comprehensive overviews of their policies at their fingertips. These advancements also made complex IUL features easier to manage and understand, broadening the market to individuals who would otherwise find such financial products opaque or intimidating.

Moreover, the growing emphasis on personalized financial solutions has ushered in an age where IULs are not just a static product, but part of a larger, tailored financial strategy. Financial advisors and planners now incorporate IULs into elaborate retirement and estate planning solutions, demonstrating their capacity for both immediate protection and long-term growth.

In summary, the evolution of IUL as a financial tool reflects a broader trend of financial products adapting to consumer demand for flexibility, growth opportunity, and protection. What started as a novel insurance solution in the 1990s has become a staple in sophisticated financial planning, offering a dynamic blend of insurance and investment-like qualities. As we continue to navigate the complexities of modern financial landscapes, the adaptability and multifaceted benefits of IUL policies ensure their durability as a cornerstone in wealth-building strategies.

The Tax Advantages of Indexed Universal Life (IUL) Policies

In the complex landscape of financial planning and wealth management, tax-efficiency remains a paramount concern for individuals and families striving to maximize their financial potential. Indexed Universal Life (IUL) insurance policies present an intriguing proposition in this regard, offering unique tax advantages that can significantly enhance one's financial strategy. This subpoint delves into the tax benefits associated with IUL policies, providing a detailed exploration of how they stand out compared to other investment vehicles.

First and foremost, the cash value growth within an IUL policy is tax-deferred. This means that policyholders do not pay taxes on the growth of their policy's cash value until it is withdrawn. This deferred taxation allows the cash value to compound over time without the drag of taxes, potentially leading to substantial growth. This is akin to the benefits seen in retirement accounts like IRAs or 401(k)s, but with the added flexibility and benefits that life insurance policies provide.

Additionally, one of the most compelling tax advantages of IULs lies in the ability to withdraw funds on a tax-free basis. Policyholders can access their cash value through policy loans, which are not considered taxable events. As long as the policy remains in force, and the loans are managed properly, individuals can leverage this feature to supplement retirement income or fund other financial needs without incurring income taxes. This is a crucial advantage over traditional investment accounts, such as stocks or mutual funds, where selling shares typically triggers a taxable event.

Furthermore, IUL policies offer the opportunity to transfer wealth to beneficiaries in a tax-efficient manner. The death benefit from an IUL policy is generally passed on to heirs' income-tax-free. This aspect of IUL policies is particularly appealing for individuals looking to leave a legacy while minimizing the tax burden on their beneficiaries. It allows the policyholder to effectively plan for intergenerational wealth transfer, which can significantly impact the financial security of future generations.

Another noteworthy tax advantage of IUL policies is the ability to potentially circumvent estate taxes. When structured properly, the death benefits from an IUL policy can be excluded from the policyholder's estate, thereby reducing the overall estate tax liability. This is particularly beneficial for high-net-worth individuals who might otherwise face significant estate taxes. By using an irrevocable life insurance trust (ILIT) or other advanced estate planning techniques, the policyholder can ensure that the proceeds from an IUL policy pass on to beneficiaries without being subjected to federal estate taxation.

In comparison to other investment vehicles, such as mutual funds or real estate, IUL policies stand out due to their combination of life insurance protection and tax-advantaged growth. While mutual funds can offer significant growth potential, they are subject to capital gains taxes when assets are sold, and dividend distributions are typically taxed annually. Real estate investments, on the other hand, can provide tax deductions through depreciation, but also come with their own set of tax obligations and complexities. IUL policies offer a streamlined alternative, combining the benefits of insurance and tax-optimized wealth accumulation in one package.

It's important to note, however, that the tax benefits of IUL policies are best realized when the policy is used as part of a comprehensive financial strategy. Policyholders must be diligent about managing loans and withdrawals to ensure the policy does not lapse, which could trigger tax liabilities. Additionally, the costs associated with policy premiums and the complexities of contract terms necessitate careful planning and consultation with financial advisors or tax professionals.

In conclusion, the tax advantages of IUL policies provide a powerful incentive for individuals seeking to optimize their financial strategies. By offering tax-deferred growth, tax-free loan access, and favorable tax treatment for death benefits, IULs can serve as a cornerstone in a well-rounded financial plan. These advantages, coupled with the lifetime coverage and flexibility of the policies, position IULs as a compelling option for those looking to enhance their wealth-building potential while navigating the intricacies of tax obligations. As with any financial instrument, a thorough understanding and strategic implementation are key to harnessing the full potential of what IUL policies have to offer.

Illustrating IUL Benefits Through Scenarios

To grasp the multifaceted benefits of Indexed Universal Life (IUL) insurance, it is instrumental to examine illustrative scenarios that showcase its potential as a wealth-building tool. By delving into real-world applications, one can appreciate the versatility and value that IUL policies offer to policyholders across various stages of life and financial goals.

Scenario 1: The Long-Term Wealth Builder

Consider John, a 35-year-old financial advisor who understands the importance of diversifying his investment portfolio. John wants to secure a portion of his financial future while ensuring his loved ones are financially protected. He opts for an IUL policy, recognizing its dual benefit of providing life insurance coverage and the potential for cash value accumulation. By directing his policy's cash value to track a market index such as the S&P 500, John taps into the potential for higher returns, while still enjoying the IUL's built-in safety net during market downturns due to its floor rate of zero percent—ensuring that his principal investment isn't eroded by negative market movements.

Over the decades, John's IUL policy has grown along with the market, benefiting from the upside potential thanks to the index-linking feature. By retirement, John accesses the policy's accumulated cash value tax-free, using it as a supplemental retirement income. This scenario highlights the IUL's capacity for long-term growth, tax advantages, and risk mitigation, combining to create a robust strategy for wealth accumulation and security.

Scenario 2: The Tax-Conscious Entrepreneur

Next, envision Sarah, a 45-year-old entrepreneur who owns a thriving small business. Given the fluctuating nature of the business landscape, Sarah is keen on cultivating a financial strategy that allows flexibility and liquidity while minimizing her tax burden. She invests in an IUL policy, thereby not only ensuring she has death benefit protection but also incorporating a tax-advantaged vehicle into her financial planning.

Sarah contributes diligently to her IUL, leveraging it as a financial reservoir that can be drawn upon for business expansion opportunities, emergency situations, or as a bridge fund during lean periods. The ability to take policy loans against the cash value without triggering a taxable event provides Sarah with financial maneuverability. This aspect of IUL policies starkly contrasts with the tax implications tied to liquidating other types of investment accounts prematurely. Through this scenario, we see how IULs can cater to the needs of modern entrepreneurs by aligning financial protection with strategically accessible wealth.

Scenario 3: The Legacy Planner

Finally, let's examine the case of Margaret and Richard, a couple in their 60s approaching their golden years with a desire to leave a meaningful legacy for their children and grandchildren. After analyzing various options, they choose an IUL policy to solidify their estate planning efforts. The death benefit component ensures that when they pass on, their beneficiaries will receive a substantial tax-free inheritance, which can be used to pay estate taxes, settle debts, or as a financial boon for future generations.

Moreover, during their lifetime, Margaret and Richard utilize the growing cash value component of their IUL policy to enhance their retirement lifestyle while also maintaining the assurance that their policy will likely continue accumulating with an upward market trajectory. The guaranteed death benefit, coupled with the tax-free access to the policy's cash value, becomes a cornerstone of their financial strategy, providing peace of mind and certainty in legacy planning.

These scenarios underline the strategic advantages that Indexed Universal Life insurance can offer to various demographics. Whether one is seeking long-term growth and retirement security, financial agility for business endeavors, or legacy planning, an IUL policy can be a pivotal component of a well-rounded financial strategy. Understanding these scenarios provides a clearer picture of how IULs can be tailored to meet individual needs, offering both protection and potential for growth in a tax-efficient manner. As such, Indexed Universal Life insurance continues to be a powerful, adaptable tool that complements diverse financial planning objectives.

Challenges and Considerations in Choosing IUL

When contemplating the inclusion of an Indexed Universal Life (IUL) insurance policy within your financial strategy, a multitude of factors demand careful attention. The allure of IUL policies lies in their ability to serve dual functions of providing life insurance coverage along with an investment component tied to market indices. However, this multifaceted nature introduces a variety of challenges that should be meticulously considered to ensure the alignment of an IUL with your personal financial goals and risk tolerance.

Understanding the Complexity of IUL Policies

At the core of the challenges associated with IUL policies is their inherent complexity. Unlike term life insurance, which is straightforward in its offer of a death benefit for a specified period, IUL policies encompass a more intricate structure. They combine elements of life insurance with equity indexing, which requires a grasp of both insurance dynamics and market index performance. The policy's cash value growth is tied to the performance of a market index such as the S&P 500. However, it's crucial to recognize that these policies do not partake directly in the stock market. Instead, they offer the growth potential based on an index's performance while providing a safety net against market declines.

The variety of features—such as cap rates, participation rates, and floors—render IUL policies quite intricate. Each of these elements can significantly influence the growth of the policy's cash value. For instance, cap rates limit the maximum return the cash value can earn, regardless of how well the underlying index performs. Understanding these terms and how they interact is crucial for prospective policyholders, as they impact the potential for wealth accumulation within the policy.

Cost Structure and Fees

Another consideration is the cost structure associated with IUL policies. These insurance products are not devoid of costs, and those costs can erode potential returns. Charges typically include the cost of insurance, administration fees, surrender charges, and management fees for the policy's cash account. Ensuring that you have a clear understanding of these costs and how they are levied is essential. These expenses can differ significantly across different policies and insurers, affecting the overall value proposition of the IUL policy.

Moreover, considering the duration over which you intend to keep the policy is an important factor. IUL policies are generally designed as long-term financial vehicles. Surrendering a policy early can lead to significant financial penalties, impacting the policyholder's long-term financial plan. This calls for a robust due diligence process and a profound understanding of the policy's terms and conditions, specifically regarding the surrender periods and associated charges.

Assessing Your Financial Goals and Risk Tolerance

Choosing an IUL policy must be in concert with a comprehensive assessment of your financial goals and risk tolerance. IUL policies can offer a valuable blend of protection and cash accumulation; however, this depends entirely on the policy structure and the individual's financial objectives. A clear articulation of your financial goals is crucial. For instance, if your aim is to provide a financial legacy to your heirs while simultaneously building cash value that can be accessed tax-free during retirement, an IUL policy might be suitable.

The risk tolerance of the policyholder also plays a pivotal role. While IUL policies offer downside protection through a guaranteed minimum interest rate, they also limit upside potential with cap rates. This structure is advantageous for those who are risk-averse and prefer some degree of certainty but may not appeal to those willing to take higher risks for potentially greater rewards. Understanding how your risk tolerance aligns with the inherent product features of an IUL policy is vital in making an informed decision.

Advisory Support and Professional Guidance

Given the complexities and nuances involved, engaging with knowledgeable financial advisors or insurance professionals is imperative when considering an IUL policy. These experts can provide valuable insights and help decipher the myriads of terms and conditions associated with IUL policies, tailoring their advice to fit your unique financial situation and goals. However, selecting the right advisor is equally crucial; it requires due diligence to ensure they possess the requisite expertise and operate with your best interests in mind.

Market and Policy Provider Evaluation

Finally, the choice of the insurance company offering the IUL policy should not be overlooked.

Insurer reputation, financial stability, and track record in managing IUL products are vital factors to consider. The differences in policy features offered by various insurers can significantly affect the policy's performance and stability. Therefore, a comparative analysis of options across multiple insurers might reveal substantial differences that can impact long-term financial outcomes.

In conclusion, while Indexed Universal Life insurance offers enticing benefits, including tax advantages and growth potential linked to market indices, it requires a thorough evaluation of its challenges and considerations. By understanding the complexity, costs, and alignment with personal financial goals, policyholders can harness the full potential of IUL policies as part of a diversified financial strategy.

Chapter 2: Maximizing Tax-Free Income Potential

Strategies for Accessing Tax-Free Income through Policy Loans and Withdrawals

When discussing the potential of Indexed Universal Life (IUL) policies as a source of tax-free income, one must delve into the intricacies of policy loans and withdrawals. These mechanisms are pivotal in allowing policyholders to harness the cash value appreciation of their IUL policies without triggering immediate taxation or penalties, making them a crucial part of a comprehensive financial strategy.

Understanding Policy Loans

One of the standout features of an IUL policy is the ability to take out a policy loan. Policy loans are essentially a borrowing against the cash value that has built up within the life insurance contract. This is not unlike borrowing against the equity in a home; however, it boasts a crucial advantage – tax efficiency. When you execute a policy loan, you are not withdrawing the funds directly from your cash value but instead using it as collateral. This distinction is vital because it allows the amount borrowed to remain untouched by taxation, as you are not technically realizing any gains.

Loan Mechanics and Terms

The mechanics of a policy loan are straightforward. The life insurance company lends a portion of the cash value to the policyholder and charges interest on this loan. The interest rates on these loans can vary and are generally set by the insurance company, often influenced by prevailing market rates. Some policies offer variable interest rates, while others are fixed, giving policyholders predictability in planning their financial outlay.

Importantly, interest paid on the loan accrues within the policy, impacting on the available cash value. If left unchecked, unpaid interest can compound and potentially reduce the future available cash value or death benefit. Despite this, many policyholders favor policy loans because the cost of borrowing can often be offset by the continued growth of the underlying cash value, especially if market conditions are favorable.

Strategic Utilization of Policy Loans

Policy loans are predominantly beneficial when policyholders need supplemental income but wish to preserve their policy's value, as these loans allow for liquidity without a requirement to alter the policy's cash value directly. Situations such as funding retirement, financing a major purchase, or providing temporary liquidity during a financial setback are ideal occasions for leveraging a policy loan.

Exploring Withdrawals

In contrast to taking a loan, a withdrawal entails directly tapping into the cash value of the policy. While generally still tax-free up to the amount of premiums paid (known as the cost basis), withdrawals can have a more immediate impact on the policy's cash value and death benefit than loans.

Impact of Withdrawals on Policy Value

Withdrawals reduce the cash value on a dollar-for-dollar basis and subsequently may decrease the death benefit. Beyond exhausting the cost basis, additional withdrawals may lead to tax consequences, specifically if the total withdrawals and loans exceed the amount paid in premiums, thereby entering gain territory.

In addition, frequent or significant withdrawals can risk lapsing the policy if not managed properly, emphasizing the need for strategic planning and thorough understanding by policyholders.

Optimal Scenarios for Withdrawals

Withdrawals are most advantageous when a policyholder desires to minimize future obligations, such as interest payments that come with loans. They may also appeal to those who need a large sum for a discrete financial goal or for emergencies that justify the associated risks, such as potential reduction in benefits.

Balancing Loans and Withdrawals

Deciding between a policy loan and a withdrawal involves weighing several factors, including the immediate financial needs, the ongoing purpose of the IUL policy, and the policyholder's long-term financial goals. Generally, if the goal is to maintain the integrity of both the cash value and the future death benefit, a loan may be preferable. Conversely, if minimizing debt is prioritized or when exceeding the basis significantly risks tax implications, a withdrawal could be more suitable.

In conclusion, the appeal of using policy loans and withdrawals lies in their flexibility and tax advantages. Crafting a sound strategy involves aligning these tools with broader financial goals, understanding the impact they will have on the policy's continued performance, and navigating the inherent trade-offs to maximize the long-term benefits. Whether utilized alone or in tandem, these options provide the policyholder with a powerful means of accessing funds while maintaining a robust and effective IUL policy.

In-Depth Tax Implications of Policy Loans and Withdrawals

Expanding from the fundamentals, it's crucial to delve into the tax implications associated with policy loans and withdrawals from Indexed Universal Life (IUL) insurance. This understanding not only equips IUL policyholders to maximize their financial strategy but also ensures they navigate the tax landscape effectively, making the most out of their IUL policy without encountering unexpected tax liabilities.

Tax Treatment of Policy Loans

At the heart of the tax advantages of IUL policies are policy loans. Policy loans are a unique mechanism within IUL policies that allow policyholders to access the cash value accumulated without triggering a taxable event. The fundamental reason why policy loans are generally tax-free lies in their classification. When you take a policy loan from your IUL, you are technically borrowing against the policy's death benefit, not withdrawing your investment or gains. This means the Internal Revenue Service (IRS) does not view this as a distribution of income, and hence, it remains untaxed.

The underlying principle is straightforward: because the loan is collateralized by the death benefit, you're not diminishing the policy's death benefit unless the loan, along with any accrued interest, remains unpaid at the time of the policyholder's death. In this scenario, the death benefit is reduced by the outstanding loan amount, but during your lifetime, the borrowed amount is tax-free. This method offers an attractive means to access funds for various purposes, as it doesn't require liquidating assets or generating reportable income.

However, savvy policyholders must remember that while loans offer a tax-free access route to cash value, they are not without their considerations. Interest accrues on policy loans, and if left unpaid, this interest will be added to the loan balance. If the cumulative loan exceeds the policy's cash value, the policy could lapse, potentially transforming the loan into a taxable distribution. Thus, it's crucial to manage these loans judiciously.

Tax Treatment of Withdrawals

When it comes to withdrawals, the tax scenario differs slightly. Withdrawals from an IUL policy are generally governed by the FIFO (First In, First Out) accounting method. Under FIFO, the premium payments made to the policy are considered to be withdrawn first. Consequently, as long as withdrawals do not exceed the total amount of premiums paid, they are tax-free. This concept treats the initial withdrawals as a return of the principal, which is not taxed, as it doesn't represent profit or gain.

When policyholders withdraw amounts surpassing the total premiums paid, implications change. These excess withdrawals are viewed as taxable income by the IRS, as they are considered to be a part of the policy's earnings or growth. This potential taxable event is crucial to understand for policyholders considering larger withdrawals for significant financial needs.

Combining Loans and Withdrawals Strategically

The strategy of utilizing withdrawals in combination with loans can offer a balanced approach to accessing one's IUL's cash value. For example, a policyholder might choose to withdraw funds up to their total premium payments to avoid taxes and then switch to policy loans for additional funding needs. This combined approach requires careful planning and ongoing policy management to ensure that the policy remains healthy and sustainable over the long term.

Modified Endowment Contracts (MECs)

Moreover, understanding the tax nuances related to Modified Endowment Contracts

(MECs) is vital for policyholders. If a policy is inadvertently converted into a MEC due to excessive funding, the tax treatment of distributions changes considerably. Under a MEC, distributions are taxed as income to the extent of the policy's gain and may also incur a 10% penalty if distributed before age 59½. This makes it critical for policyholders to monitor their funding levels and ensure compliance with MEC guidelines to preserve the tax advantage of withdrawals and policy loans.

In summary, navigating the tax implications of loans and withdrawals within an IUL policy requires a careful, methodical approach. By leveraging the loan provisions for tax-free cash access and employing a FIFO strategy for withdrawals, policyholders can efficiently meet their financial goals while preserving the tax-advantaged status of their IUL. Recognizing the potential taxable triggers and understanding the implications of factors such as MECs is part of a comprehensive strategy for optimizing the benefits of an IUL policy. Through informed decision-making and strategic policy management, policyholders can harness these tools' full potential to support both immediate and long-term financial objectives.

Illustrative Examples and Case Studies

One of the most compelling aspects of Indexed Universal Life (IUL) insurance is its ability to provide tax-free income streams, a feature that is not merely theoretical but has been successfully leveraged by countless policyholders to achieve their financial goals. Through illustrative examples and real-world case studies, we can explore how IUL policies are uniquely positioned to offer financial stability and flexibility across various stages of life.

Example 1: Funding Children's Education

Consider the case of Maria, a savvy financial planner with two young children. Understanding the soaring costs of education, Maria opted to secure an IUL policy when her children were very young. Over the years, the cash value of her IUL policy grew significantly, tied to the performance of a market index but protected from market downturns due to the policy's design. When her eldest was ready to head off to university, Maria began borrowing from the accumulated cash value of her policy.

These policy loans were not only tax-free but also did not require immediate repayment, providing Maria with the flexibility she needed to manage the expenses of tuition, books, and accommodation. This strategic move allowed her to preserve her other investment portfolios, avoiding the tax implications and potential penalties often associated with traditional retirement accounts like 401(k)s or IRAs when accessed early. Maria's foresight in leveraging her IUL policy enabled her children to graduate debt-free, setting them up for financial success and allowing her to maintain her financial integrity.

Example 2: Bridging Income Gaps During Retirement

Another powerful application of IUL policies is in bridging income gaps during retirement. Take the example of John and Sarah, a couple who entered retirement sooner than expected due to a sudden health issue that forced John to leave his job early. With John no longer contributing to their household income, they needed a way to supplement their earnings without incurring additional tax burdens.

Fortunately, John had established an IUL policy decades earlier, consistently contributing premiums that built up substantial cash value over time. As they navigated this unexpected transition into retirement, John and Sarah leveraged the tax-free policy loans to cover their living expenses. This strategy allowed them to defer claiming Social Security benefits, which continued to increase in value each year they delayed, setting them up for a stronger financial position in the later years of retirement.

Example 3: Enhancing Estate Planning

For policyholders like David, an entrepreneur approaching retirement, IUL policies offer another layer of financial utility: estate planning. David proactively used his IUL policy to create a source of tax-free income, which he accessed to lower the taxable estate he would pass on to his heirs. By taking tax-free loans against the cash value of his IUL, David effectively reduced the size of his estate while still offering substantial financial support to his family.

At the same time, the IUL policy's death benefit remained intact and tax-free, thus ensuring that his beneficiaries received a legacy without the burdens some inheritance methods might impose. This strategic use of an IUL policy allowed David to control the allocation of his wealth with a high degree of tax efficiency, providing financial freedom and security for both himself and those he cared about.

Example 4: Safeguarding Against Market Volatility

An additional real-world application can be seen in the case of Linda, a cautious investor who was wary of market volatility. She opted for an IUL policy for its principal protection feature, which meant her cash value would never decrease due to negative index performance. This decision was particularly prudent during the financial downturn, where many saw the value of their investments in traditional stock markets plummet.

Over the years, Linda's IUL policy provided a stable growth avenue. As she approached retirement, she was able to begin taking tax-free loans against her policy, safely knowing that her principal remained unscathed and could continue to earn interest. By capitalizing on the benefits of her IUL, she protected herself from the financial instabilities that caught many off guard, securing both her present and future financial wellbeing.

These examples illustrate the diverse ways in which Indexed Universal Life insurance policies can be strategically utilized to generate tax-free income streams. By planning ahead and leveraging the unique features of IULs, policyholders have the potential to fund educational expenses, bridge retirement income gaps, enhance estate planning, and safeguard against market risks—all while benefiting from the exceptional tax advantages these policies offer. This practical knowledge empowers individuals to incorporate IULs into their broader financial strategies, ensuring resilience and success in meeting their financial ambitions.

Impact of Tax Legislation on IUL Policyholders

The relationship between tax legislation and Indexed Universal Life (IUL) policyholders is a dynamic interplay that is constantly evolving.

63

Understanding how recent changes in tax laws impact the advantages of IUL products is crucial for any policyholder intent on maximizing their financial benefits. As tax policies shift, adjustments in tax brackets, estate tax thresholds, and other relevant changes often require policyholders to reassess their strategies to ensure compliance while maintaining the policy's desirable tax-free income benefits.

Recent Tax Legislation: Changes and Implications

Key revisions in tax legislation over the past few years have had significant impacts on IUL policyholders. Changes in tax brackets, for instance, directly affect the amount of disposable income individuals have and, by extension, their capacity to invest in or borrow against their IUL policies. In particular, lower tax rates for certain income groups may increase the disposable income available, allowing more flexibility in premium payments and additional contributions to build cash value.

The estate tax threshold is another critical factor. Recently, there has been a trend toward increasing the estate tax exclusion amounts, which has implications for IUL policies. A higher exclusion amount allows more wealth to be transferred without incurring estate taxes, making IUL's tax-free death benefit even more attractive for policyholders looking to use the policy as a wealth transfer mechanism. Moreover, the benefits of avoiding estate taxes through the strategic use of an IUL policy cannot be understated, as these changes can significantly affect the net wealth transferred to the next generation.

Another aspect of recent tax legislation that impacts IULs is the changes regarding the deductibility of certain items and contributions. For instance, changes that impact the deductibility of interest on policy loans can affect those who use policy loans against IULs as a source of tax-free income. Understanding these nuances is crucial, as they can change the underlying calculus of the financial strategies associated with IULs.

Anticipated Legislative Trends

Looking ahead, several potential legislative changes may impact IUL policyholders. One such trend is the likelihood of fluctuating tax brackets, which could swing either upwards or downwards in response to economic conditions. Policyholders may find that their taxable income projections shift, necessitating closer monitoring and potentially adjusting premium payments or loan strategies to accommodate these changes.

There is also ongoing discussion about modifying the way life insurance policies are treated under estate tax laws. While it is not currently law, any move to include more IUL benefits within the taxable estate could alter how policyholders approach estate planning. This would necessitate strategies to mitigate potential impacts, such as utilizing gifts or trusts to manage the distribution of assets more effectively.

Furthermore, discussions about tax reform at the congressional level could introduce new tax benefits or eliminate existing ones. For IUL policyholders, it's essential to stay informed about legislative measures that could redefine the tax advantages of their policies. Such changes could affect the tax deferral aspect of IULs, influencing the accumulation of cash value and the tax treatment of loans and withdrawals.

Strategic Advice for Policyholders

Given this ever-shifting landscape, policyholders should adopt a proactive approach to managing their IUL policies. Staying informed about legislative changes and working closely with a financial advisor who specializes in this domain can ensure that adjustments are made promptly to optimize the benefits of the IUL policy.

One strategic approach is to regularly review the policy and its alignment with financial goals. Such reviews should consider the impacts of any recent legislative changes, keeping an eye on how they may have shifted the strategic advantage of the policy. Analyzing performance benchmarks and looking at potential policy adjustments can help maintain the desired financial outcomes.

Additionally, policyholders should consider the use of complementary financial instruments like trusts or annuities that can provide additional layers of tax protection and optimization. These tools can be particularly effective in estate planning and wealth transfer, ensuring that the policy's benefits are maximally leveraged in a tax-efficient manner.

In conclusion, while tax legislation will continue to evolve, the strategic use of IUL policies can provide significant opportunities for financial growth and stability. Policyholders who stay informed, adapt to legislative changes, and employ strategic foresight will be well-positioned to continue reaping the tax-free income benefits offered by their IUL policies.

Aligning IUL Strategies with Long-term Financial Goals

Indexed Universal Life (IUL) policies have become an invaluable tool in the arsenal of savvy financial planners, offering a strategic pathway to balance the need for protection with the ambitious goals of wealth accumulation, retirement security, and legacy building. Policyholders who meticulously align their IUL strategies with their long-term financial objectives can unlock the full potential of these versatile products. It is essential to understand how to effectively incorporate tax-free withdrawals and loans from an IUL policy into a diversified financial portfolio, considering the dynamic interplay of market conditions, personal financial circumstances, and evolving life goals.

Retirement Planning

Retirement planning is often the cornerstone of long-term financial strategies. An IUL policy can be instrumental in ensuring secure retirement by providing a source of tax-free income. Unlike traditional retirement accounts such as 401(k)s or IRAs, which are subject to required minimum distributions and taxation, funds accessed from the cash value of an IUL through loans and withdrawals are typically tax-free when managed carefully. This feature is particularly advantageous for high-net-worth individuals aiming to mitigate tax liabilities in their retirement years.

For retirees, the predictability and flexibility offered by IUL can be indispensable. By planning withdrawals and loans during favorable market conditions, policyholders can sustain their lifestyle without depleting their nest egg. Additionally, the death benefit feature of the IUL policy enhances retirement planning by providing a financial cushion for surviving family members or fulfilling philanthropic goals.

Wealth Accumulation

IUL policies are also fertile ground for wealth accumulation, thanks to their unique design that combines life insurance with an investment component. By linking the cash value to a market index, policyholders can benefit from market upswings, while enjoying protection against downturns due to built-in-floor rates. This blend allows for a gradual yet reliable growth of wealth over time. The tax-deferred nature of the cash value growth further accelerates wealth accumulation by avoiding the annual tax drag associated with other investment vehicles.

Strategically using tax-free loans and withdrawals can elevate wealth-building endeavors. Rather than dipping into taxable accounts when liquidity is needed, borrowing against the accrued cash value in an IUL policy can provide the necessary funds without triggering taxable events. When planned with foresight, these loans can support significant life investments, such as purchasing a property or funding a child's education, without disrupting the growth trajectory of other investments.

Legacy Planning

Legacy planning extends beyond mere asset management; it embodies the desire to leave a meaningful impact on future generations or chosen causes. An IUL policy, when structured smartly, can serve as a powerful legacy tool. The tax-free death benefit, potentially substantial if the policy is well-funded, ensures that beneficiaries receive financial support unencumbered by taxation. This feature not only preserves wealth but also enables policyholders to craft a legacy that aligns with their values and aspirations.

Moreover, policyholders can use the policy's cash value to make lifetime gifts without immediate tax consequences. By extracting tax-free loans from their IUL policies, individuals can provide financial support to heirs or charitable causes during their lifetime, thus witnessing the influence of their legacy firsthand.

Integrating IUL into a Diversified Portfolio

To maximize the advantages of an IUL policy, policyholders should see it as an integral part of a diversified financial portfolio. This entails a consistent review of market trends, personal financial positions, and life circumstances to identify optimal times to execute loans and withdrawals. The flexible design of IULs, including the ability to adjust premium payments and death benefit amounts, allows policyholders to adapt their strategies to meet changing needs.

For instance, during economic downturns, IUL's cash value provides a buffer that can be tapped into without selling off other investments at a loss. Conversely, during prosperous times, allowing the cash value to compound can amplify wealth accumulation, underscoring the importance of a well-timed and holistic strategy.

In conclusion, the versatility of IUL policies opens up myriad possibilities for aligning with long-term financial goals. Whether planning for a comfortable retirement, accumulating wealth, or leaving a lasting legacy, integrating an IUL policy into a well-rounded financial strategy can offer unparalleled benefits. By navigating through tax-free income avenues, policyholders can tailor their approach to suit their current and future financial landscapes, ensuring that their financial aspirations are not only met but surpassed.

Navigating Risks and Pitfalls of Accessing Cash Value

Accessing tax-free income through Indexed Universal Life (IUL) policies can be a powerful strategy for enhancing financial freedom, but it also comes with potential risks that policyholders must navigate with care. As with any financial instrument, understanding and managing these risks is crucial to maximizing the benefits while safeguarding against potential downsides. Unchecked borrowing or premature withdrawals from an IUL policy can have significant implications for both the policy and the policyholder's overall financial health.

Potential Risks: Excessive Borrowing and Premature Withdrawals

One of the key risks associated with accessing tax-free income through IUL policies is the impact of excessive borrowing. While policy loans can provide a source of tax-free income, borrowing too much against the policy's cash value can reduce the death benefit and cash value available for future use. This can be particularly problematic if the policyholder is relying on the death benefit as part of their estate planning. Excessive borrowing can also inadvertently lead to the policy lapsing if the cash value becomes insufficient to cover the policy's expenses, including the cost of insurance.

It is essential for policyholders to maintain a delicate balance between utilizing the policy's cash value and preserving the health of the policy itself. One way to mitigate the risks of excessive borrowing is to regularly review the policy's performance and ensure that there is sufficient cash value to support any outstanding loans. This can involve periodically assessing the policy's cash value growth against market conditions and adjusting the loan amounts accordingly.

Premature withdrawals can also pose significant challenges. Like policy loans, withdrawals from the policy can erode the cash value if not managed judiciously. Taking withdrawals early in the policy's life span can hinder the potential for cash value growth, limiting the overall benefits that the policyholder might expect from the IUL policy. It is crucial to weigh the immediate needs for liquidity against the long-term financial objectives to ensure that withdrawals do not hinder future financial health.

Mitigation Strategies and Best Practices

To protect against these risks, policyholders should implement the best practices that support the sustainability of their IUL policies. One such practice is setting a strategic plan for accessing the policy's cash value that aligns with long-term financial goals. This includes determining an optimal borrowing and withdrawal strategy that complements their broader financial plan, taking into account their cash flow needs, tax situation, and investment goals.

Maintaining sufficient cash value is another critical best practice. Regularly monitoring the policy's performance and making necessary adjustments—such as premium payments to bolster the cash value—can help ensure the policy remains viable and continues to provide the intended benefits. This proactive approach allows policyholders to mitigate the risks of underfunding and protect against the possibility of the policy lapsing.

It is also advisable for policyholders to ensure that their life coverage is not compromised. IUL policies are designed to offer both investment and insurance benefits, so maintaining adequate life coverage is integral to their overall value. Avoiding withdrawals or loans that significantly diminish the death benefit is crucial, particularly for those who intend to use the policy as part of a legacy or estate planning strategy.

Furthermore, engaging with a knowledgeable financial advisor can also be instrumental in managing IUL policies effectively. Financial advisors can provide personalized insights and strategies that consider the nuances of each policyholder's financial situation, including tax implications, investment goals, and risk tolerance. By collaborating with a trusted advisor, policyholders can navigate complex decisions with confidence.

Lastly, understanding the terms and conditions of the specific IUL policy is vital to avoiding common pitfalls. Each policy has unique features and restrictions, and being fully informed about these details can empower policyholders to make educated decisions about borrowing and withdrawals.

In conclusion, while accessing tax-free income through IUL policies offers substantial benefits, it requires careful management to avoid common risks and pitfalls. By maintaining sufficient cash value, ensuring adequate life coverage, and seeking professional advice when needed, policyholders can harness the full potential of their IUL policies to meet their financial goals without compromising their overall financial health.

Chapter 3: Tax-Efficient Strategies for IUL Policyholders

Understanding policy loans and withdrawals within the realm of Indexed Universal Life (IUL) insurance is crucial for anyone looking to leverage IUL as a powerful financial planning tool. These mechanisms allow policyholders to access the accumulated cash value of their policies, providing a source of tax-free income when structured properly. However, to fully appreciate the potential benefits and navigate the complexities of policy loans and withdrawals, it's essential to explore their underlying structures, benefits, and best practices.

At the heart of an IUL policy is the cash value component, which accrues over time based on index-linked crediting strategies, offering the potential for growth with downside protection. This cash value can be thought of as a reservoir of funds on which policyholders can draw. However, rather than depleting this reservoir through direct withdrawals, many opt for policy loans, an approach that maintains the growth potential of the cash value while providing liquidity.

When a policyholder takes out a loan against their IUL policy, they are essentially borrowing from the insurer against the cash value. One of the standout features of this loan is that it is generally not considered a taxable event so long as the policy remains in force. This attribute makes it an appealing strategy for individuals aiming to access funds without triggering a tax liability, provided the loan is properly managed.

The mechanics of policy loans involve the insurer using the cash value as collateral. Typically, policyholders can borrow a substantial portion of their cash value, often up to 90% or more—though this depends on the specific terms of the policy and the insurer's rules. Importantly, as long as the policyholder regularly pays the loan interest, the amount borrowed remains tax-free, allowing policyholders to strategize their income needs effectively.

Another critical element to understand is the impact of interest. Loans accrue interest, which can be either fixed or variable, depending on the policy terms. To optimize the benefits of a policy loan, it's essential to manage this interest prudently. Some policies allow for interest to be added to the loan balance, a process known as loan interest capitalization. While convenient, this can lead to a compounded increase in the total loan balance if not monitored carefully.

Policyholders must be vigilant in ensuring that loan balances do not approach or exceed the cash value. Doing so can avoid the policy lapse, which could trigger tax consequences and loss of coverage. Regularly reviewing the policy with a knowledgeable financial advisor can help prevent such scenarios and ensure the policy continues to meet financial goals.

Withdrawals, on the other hand, involve taking out a portion of the policy's cash value directly. Unlike loans, withdrawals reduce the cash value and death benefit immediately. Initially, these withdrawals can be tax-free, as long as the amount does not exceed the total premiums paid into the policy, known as the basis. Beyond this, withdrawals can become taxable, and the reduction in cash value might potentially affect the policy's performance and its ability to sustain ongoing charges.

Strategically, a combination of loans and withdrawals can be used to create a diversified approach to accessing the cash value. For example, policyholders might rely on withdrawals up to the cost basis, ensuring no tax impact initially, and then switch to loans for additional liquidity needs. This strategy allows for the maximization of tax efficiency while managing the impacts on the cash value and policy sustainability.

Moreover, it is critically important for policyholders to maintain a vigilant approach in monitoring the health of their IUL policies. Periodical reviews and adjustments, often in consultation with specialized financial advisors, can ensure that the policy remains aligned with personal financial goals and adapts to any changes in circumstances or broader economic conditions.

Policy loans and withdrawals are powerful tools embedded within Indexed Universal Life insurance policies. They offer flexibility, liquidity, and tax advantages when used strategically. Understanding their functions, limitations, and best application practices empower policyholders to harness the full potential of their IUL policies, turning them into vital components of a broader financial and retirement planning strategy. With careful planning and oversight, the accessibility of IUL's cash value can offer substantial financial advantages, providing a reliable stream of funds poised to support various life goals while safeguarding wealth efficiently and effectively.

Impact of Tax Laws on IUL Policyholders

Navigating the labyrinth of tax laws is crucial to effectively managing and maximizing the benefits of an Indexed Universal Life (IUL) insurance policy. Understanding the interplay between tax legislation and IUL can dramatically impact how policyholders approach their financial strategies. This section will explore the significant tax implications that IUL policyholders should be aware of, providing clarity on how current tax laws shape the advantages offered by these versatile financial instruments.

Tax-Deferred Growth

One of the most compelling aspects of IUL policies is the opportunity for tax-deferred growth. The cash value within an IUL policy grows based on index-linked credits, such as the S&P 500, without being subjected to annual taxation on the earnings. This tax deferral allows the policyholder's investment within the policy to compound more efficiently, as taxes are not eroding the gains each year. Current U.S. tax laws continue to uphold this advantage, allowing policyholders to accelerate their wealth accumulation within the policy. This is a notable benefit when compared to other investment vehicles that might incur annual capital gains taxes.

Tax-Free Policy Loans

Policyholders can leverage the tax-free loan feature of IUL policies, a distinctive mechanism allowed by tax regulations. When a policyholder takes out a loan against their policy's cash value, the IRS does not regard this action as a taxable event, given that it is technically not a withdrawal of funds, but rather a borrowing against their own money. This provision allows for liquidity while avoiding the incurrence of taxable income. It's a strategic method for policyholders to access funds efficiently, whether it's for supplementing retirement income, funding a major purchase, or addressing emergency needs.

Modified Endowment Contract (MEC)

However, policyholders must exercise caution to avoid their IUL policy being classified as a Modified Endowment Contract (MEC). The Technical and Miscellaneous Revenue Act of 1988 (TAMRA) established rules to prevent life insurance policies from being primarily investment vehicles rather than life insurance. Policies classified as MECs lose the tax advantages of traditional life insurance contracts — specifically, loans and withdrawals become taxable, and they may also incur a 10% penalty if the policyholder is under age 59½. To avoid MEC status, policyholders should work closely with their insurance specialists to manage premium payments and ensure the policy continues to meet the requirements that define it as life insurance under IRS guidelines.

Tax-Advantaged Death Benefit

An IUL policy is perhaps best known for its capability to deliver a tax-free death benefit to beneficiaries. Under federal tax law, the death benefit received by beneficiaries is generally income-tax-free, which enables policyholders to efficiently leave a financial legacy without imposing a tax burden. Legislative changes have maintained this benefit as a vital estate-planning tool. However, policyholders should be wary of potential changes in estate tax laws that could affect wealth transfer strategies and periodically review their policies to ensure they align with current regulations.

Contributions and Withdrawal Implications

While the contributions made to an IUL policy are non-deductible, the strategic focus lies in the powerful and flexible tax-free features accessible throughout the policy's maturity. Partial withdrawals of cash value are generally not taxable up to the amount of the premiums paid into the policy, known as the policy's cost basis. Understanding these tax implications can help policyholders withdraw funds strategically, minimizing tax liabilities while still benefiting from the policy's many advantages.

Impact on Future Tax Reforms

Policyholders must remain vigilant about prospective tax reforms that could alter the landscape of tax benefits linked to IUL policies. Tax laws are subject to change, and policyholders should be prepared to adapt their strategies accordingly. Working with a knowledgeable financial advisor who understands the intricacies of life insurance and tax law will help mitigate any adverse impacts from legislative changes.

In conclusion, while the landscape of U.S. tax law remains complex, it continues to offer numerous advantages for IUL policyholders. By leveraging the tax-deferred and tax-free components of a policy, while avoiding pitfalls like MEC status, policyholders can skillfully navigate their IUL policies to align with broader financial goals. Remaining informed and proactive will ensure that taxpayers derive the most out of their investments, effectively coupling the growth potential of index markets with the security and advantages of tax legislation.

Strategic Use of Policy Loans to Achieve Financial Goals

Indexed Universal Life (IUL) insurance policies offer a unique financial lever for individuals seeking to align their life insurance strategies with broader financial goals. One of the most compelling features of an IUL policy is its ability to generate tax-free income through policy loans. This strategy, when used judiciously, can effectively serve as a financial bridge, supporting both short-term needs and long-term aspirations.

Understanding Policy Loans

At the heart of the strategy to access the cash value of your IUL policy are policy loans. Unlike traditional loans, which can entail lengthy approval processes and strict repayment structures, policy loans are straightforward and flexible. The mechanics are simple: you borrow against the accumulated cash value in your policy. As the cash value in IUL grows based on indexed market performance, this nest egg can be tapped into through these loans.

One of the key benefits of such loans is their tax-free nature. As long as the policy remains in force, you can take out loans against the cash value without tax implications, providing an effective means to access liquidity while still preserving your policy's benefits and without triggering taxable events.

Flexible Use of Funds

Policy loans can be strategically employed to meet a variety of financial goals. This flexibility is one of the most appealing aspects of IUL policy loans.

1. Education Funding: Parents and grandparents often utilize policy loans to fund education expenses for their children or grandchildren. By using a policy loan, they avoid the tax hits that often accompany dipping into traditional investment accounts or selling off assets. The policy loan can be repaid on your schedule or not at all—since any unpaid loans will simply reduce the death benefit.

2. Business Investment: For entrepreneurs and business owners, IUL policy loans can serve as a source of capital to finance business expansions or cover lean periods. Unlike business loans from financial institutions, these do not require proof of income or impeccable credit scores, making them an attractive option for those needing quick and easy access to funds.

3. Retirement Supplementation: Leveraging policy loans as a means of supplementing retirement income is a prudent strategy for policyholders. These loans can provide a tax-free supplement to social security or other retirement income, allowing retirees to maintain their lifestyle without tapping into other taxed accounts.

Preserving Wealth and Legacy

An essential consideration while taking policy loans is understanding the implications on the policy's death benefit. While policy loans can reduce the death benefit, effective management ensures that this reduction is minimized.

1. Managing Loan Balances: It is crucial to monitor the balance of any policy loans and assess the strategy regarding repayment. Regular interest payments can help manage the accrued interest, ensuring the loan balance does not significantly detract from the death benefit over time.

2. Creating a Legacy: Many policyholders are concerned about preserving their estate and ensuring that they leave a meaningful legacy. Strategic management of policy loans can ensure that the short-term cash needs do not

significantly detract from the financial benefits passed on to beneficiaries.

Maximizing Financial Goals

When strategically and judiciously taking out policy loans, it's essential to maintain a balance between immediate financial needs and prospective policy growth.

- Periodic Review: Regular review with a financial advisor or insurance expert is vital. Policies and market conditions change, and what might have been a suitable strategy two years ago could need adjustment today.

- Holistic Financial Planning: Integrating policy loans within a comprehensive financial strategy ensures that short-term cash flow is balanced with long-term growth, providing the policyholder with a sense of financial security.

- Understand Policy Illustrations and Projections: By accurately interpreting policy illustrations, policyholders can discern future growth patterns and potential flexibility levels available at various stages of life.

In conclusion, the strategic use of policy loans from an IUL is a tailor-made approach for leveraging policy benefits while advancing financial goals. It encapsulates a method for balancing the need for immediate liquidity with the preservation of long-term wealth and legacy planning. Policyholders who approach these financial tools with a strategic mindset can navigate present needs and future ambitions with greater ease and assurance, ultimately using their policies to their maximum advantage.

Tax-Free Income for Retirement Planning

For those planning their retirement, the promise of tax-free income is an alluring prospect. Indexed Universal Life (IUL) insurance policies present a compelling strategy in this regard. By utilizing specific features inherent to IULs, policyholders can access the cash value of their policies tax-free, providing a robust financial tool in retirement planning. This strategy, when applied wisely, can alleviate tax burdens during retirement, preserving wealth and improving financial security.

To understand how IULs offer tax-free retirement income, it is essential to unpack the dynamics of policy loans and withdrawals, which are core to leveraging the policy's cash value. Unlike withdrawals from traditional retirement accounts such as 401(k)s or IRAs, where distributions are typically subject to income tax, IUL policy loans and withdrawals can be structured to avoid taxation. The key lies in obtaining loans against the policy rather than withdrawing the cash value directly.

When a policyholder takes a loan against their IUL, they are essentially borrowing from the policy's cash value. This transaction is not considered taxable income because it is a loan with the intention of repayment, despite the fact that it may not need to be repaid during the policyholder's lifetime. Interest on these loans is often offset by the interest earned on the policy's cash value, especially if the policy is structured correctly with the assistance of a knowledgeable advisor. This strategic borrowing offers a mechanism to draw on the accumulated cash value of the tax-free policy, providing a stream of income that can support various needs in retirement.

Moreover, IULs offer a level of flexibility rarely found in other financial products. If managed prudently, policyholders can continue to participate in market gains through the policy's index-linked crediting strategy while avoiding losses during market downturns. This feature ensures that the cash value continues to grow tax-deferred, enhancing the amount available for future tax-free withdrawals during retirement. It's essentially a financial strategy that combines the growth potential of equities with the principal protection typically associated with fixed income products.

Another benefit is the impact of compounding interest within the IUL. Over time, the cash value grows, sometimes exponentially, depending on market performance and any additional premium contributions made over time. Policyholders can leverage this growth through loans while leaving the principal untouched, ensuring that their policy continues to compound and provide potential future income sources. This creates an ongoing foundation for sustainable tax-free income in retirement.

Additionally, IULs allow for strategic planning around other retirement income sources, maximizing overall tax efficiency. For instance, retirees with an IUL might choose to delay other taxable retirement account withdrawals, such as from IRAs or 401(k)s, thus minimizing their taxable income during specific years. This strategy is particularly beneficial in managing tax brackets, especially before reaching age 73, after which Required Minimum Distributions (RMDs) from tax-deferred retirement accounts begin.

Furthermore, the tax-free income from IUL can complement Social Security benefits. By controlling income sources and reducing overall taxable income with IUL loans, retirees may avoid triggering taxes on Social Security benefits — a common issue when retirees begin drawing from tax-deferred accounts.

It's crucial to underline that while IULs offer tremendous potential, they require careful planning and management. Policyholders should work with skilled financial advisors to tailor the policy to their specific needs and risk tolerance. Advisors can guide them on appropriate premiums, loan timings, and managing potential interest costs on policy loans to optimize their income strategy for retirement.

In conclusion, IUL policies offer a potent strategy for generating tax-free income during retirement. Through careful management and expertise, policyholders can not only secure a steady income stream but also maximize the growth and efficiency of their tax-advantaged retirement planning. By understanding and applying these strategies, retirees can protect and even enhance their financial independence during their golden years, enjoying a more comfortable and financially secure retirement.

Maintaining Financial Flexibility While Protecting Policy Benefits

In the intricate world of personal finance, maintaining flexibility is often the difference between staying afloat and thriving. Indexed Universal Life (IUL) insurance serves as a multifaceted tool in this regard, offering a unique blend of security, tax advantages, and flexibility. But how do we ensure that policyholders can maintain financial flexibility while also safeguarding the policy benefits? The answer lies in understanding the nuances of policy loans, withdrawals, and the inherent design of an IUL policy.

Understanding Financial Flexibility Through IUL

One of the hallmark features of IUL policies is their ability to offer policyholders access to their cash value through tax-free loans and withdrawals. Such access can be a lifeline during times of financial need or opportunity. Whether it is funding a child's education, supplementing retirement income, or seizing a business opportunity, the ability to tap into the cash value of an IUL policy allows for substantial financial freedom.

However, with great power comes great responsibility. While this flexibility is attractive, policyholders must tactically navigate the challenges to avoid negatively impacting the policy's long-term benefits. Mishandled, accessing these funds can affect the death benefit, cash value, and even cause the policy to lapse.

Strategy for Policy Loans

IUL policy loans are generally structured so that they do not trigger a taxable event. The insurer lends the policyholder money using the policy's cash value as collateral, allowing for funds to be accessed without diminishing the policy's principal cash value. Policy loans typically accrue interest, which can either be paid by the policyholder or added to the loan balance.

The secret to preserving policy benefits while enjoying financial flexibility is thoughtful management of these loans:

1. Monitor Loan Interest: Regularly pay the accrued interest to prevent compounding loan debt, which could potentially surpass the cash value, causing the policy to lapse.

2. Gradual Borrowing: Avoid borrowing the entire cash value. By keeping a substantial portion intact, the policy continues to compound over time and grows, providing more resources in the future.

3. Strategic Repayment: Paying back loans when possible, ensures the policy's cash value and death benefits are preserved or even improved. This can be managed strategically over time, using other financial resources or unexpected windfalls.

Navigating Policy Withdrawals

IUL policies also allow for tax-free withdrawals of cash value up to the amount of premiums paid, thanks to the FIFO (First In, First Out) taxation mechanism applied to these contracts. This means your initial contributions can be withdrawn before any gains are accessed, maintaining a tax-free status for many withdrawals.

However, strategic withdrawal management is pivotal:

1. Plan Withdrawals: Like loans, withdrawals need to be part of a broader financial strategy. Random or frequent withdrawals can diminish the death benefit over time.

2. Preserve Growth Potential: Be mindful of how the withdrawal affects the total cash value and its subsequent earnings potential. Higher remaining cash values tend to accumulate more significant returns over time due to compounding.

3. Watch for Policy Thresholds: Withdrawals should not reduce the policy value below the amount needed to cover ongoing costs and charges, which can affect its viability and benefits.

Balancing Flexibility and Protection

In a well-managed IUL policy, the dual objectives of financial flexibility and retaining policy benefits must be carefully balanced. This means understanding and anticipating potential financial needs and tying those needs to strategic financial exercises within the policy's framework.

- Integrate with Financial Goals: Map out how IUL fits within your broader financial plan—its flexibility should complement your other resources, not be the fallback option alone.

- Regular Policy Reviews: Schedule periodic reviews with your financial advisor to tweak the policy to suit evolving financial circumstances and market conditions. This ensures optimal benefits and protection are consistently aligned with personal goals.

- Understand Policy Illustrations and Projections: By accurately interpreting policy illustrations, policyholders can discern future growth patterns and potential flexibility levels available at various stages of life.

In conclusion, the strategic use of policy loans from an IUL is a tailor-made approach for leveraging policy benefits while advancing financial goals. It encapsulates a method for balancing the need for immediate liquidity with the preservation of long-term wealth and legacy planning. Policyholders who approach these financial tools with a strategic mindset can navigate present needs and future ambitions with greater ease and assurance, ultimately using their policies to their maximum advantage.

Future Trends and Predictive Changes in IUL Usage for Tax-Free Income

In the ever-evolving landscape of financial planning, Indexed Universal Life (IUL) insurance has emerged as a robust vehicle for generating tax-free income. As governmental tax policies shift and economic conditions transform, understanding future trends and predictive changes in IUL usage becomes critical for both policyholders and advisers aiming to optimize their financial strategies.

Increasing Customization and Flexibility

As the financial industry advances, customization and flexibility stand at the forefront of future IUL development. Insurers are likely to enhance policy design features, offering policyholders more personalized options tailored to their unique financial circumstances and objectives. With the ability to adjust their premium payments, death benefits, and investment options, individuals can fine-tune policies to align more closely with their long-term goals without compromising their tax-free income strategy.

Integration with Technology and Data Analytics

The integration of technology and data analytics is set to revolutionize the management and optimization of IUL policies. Insurers are increasingly leveraging artificial intelligence and big data to provide real-time insights into policy performance and market conditions. This technological shift empowers policyholders with advanced predictive analytics, allowing them to make more informed decisions about when to take loans or withdrawals, thus maximizing the tax-free benefits of their IUL policy.

Response to Regulatory Changes

With global tax regimes undergoing continual change, regulatory adaptability will be a key component of future IUL strategies. Tax legislation updates, such as changes to tax brackets or alterations in tax-advantaged saving strategies, will inevitably affect how policyholders utilize their IULs. Insurers will need to stay vigilant, updating policy structures and communication to ensure compliance and optimization under new laws while safeguarding the tax-free income aspect.

Rise in Market Volatility Management

Market volatility has always been a concern for those relying on investment vehicles to build future income. IULs offer a unique advantage here providing a combination of participation in market index gains and a protective floor against losses. As economic uncertainties persist, policyholders will increasingly value this downside protection feature. Future trends might see further refinements in participation strategies, allowing for even more precise calibration of growth potential versus risk tolerance.

Growing Awareness and Education

As more individuals become aware of the unique advantages IULs offer, there is a corresponding need for education. Financial literacy surrounding IUL policies is expected to increase, driven by both consumer demand and industry efforts. Expect to see a proliferation of resources, seminars, and advisory services aimed at demystifying IUL mechanics and their role in tax-free income planning. This growing awareness will empower more people to incorporate IULs thoughtfully into their financial portfolios.

Integration with Retirement Planning

As retirement planning evolves, there's a growing appreciation for options that ensure tax-free income streams during the post-working years. IULs are likely to become a cornerstone of retirement strategies, providing a reliable source of tax-free income through policy loans. Advisors may increasingly recommend IULs not merely as an insurance product but as a definitive retirement income planning tool, leveraging their tax advantages and flexible access to cash value.

Sustainable and Ethical Investment Options

The global shift towards sustainability and ethical investing will inevitably influence the preferences of IUL policyholders. Insurers may offer policies that align more closely with these values by providing index options focused on Environmental, Social, and Governance (ESG) criteria. Such trends will attract ethically minded consumers who are looking to grow their wealth while adhering to personal values and securing tax-free income.

The future of Indexed Universal Life insurance is poised to be one of growth and transformation, markedly driven by technological integration, regulatory responsiveness, and an increasingly savvy user base. As IULs continue to evolve, they will offer broader, more sophisticated opportunities for generating tax-free income. Policyholders armed with these insights—and the foresight to adapt to emerging trends—will find themselves at a significant advantage as they craft their financial legacies. As we look ahead, the ability to align policy features with personal and global shifts will be the hallmark of successful IUL utilization.

Chapter 4: Protecting Principal in Market Turmoil

Indexed Universal Life (IUL) policies have gained significant traction as a wealth-building tool, particularly because of their unique ability to offer downside protection during market downturns. This capability positions them as an attractive option for individuals seeking to safeguard their principal investments while still participating in market upswings. At the heart of this strategic protection are several essential mechanisms inherent within IUL policies.

Linking Cash Value Growth to Market Indexes

The cash value of an IUL policy is closely tied to the performance of a chosen stock market index, commonly the S&P 500. However, unlike direct investments in the stock market, IULs provide a protective layer against market volatility. This is achieved through a structure that allows policyholders to participate in index gains without directly exposing their cash value to market losses. The policy's cash value is credited with interest based on the positive movement of the index, while downside protection is ensured through mechanisms such as the floor rate.

The Floor Rate: A Safety Net

A defining feature of IUL policies is the floor rate, a predetermined percentage that ensures the policyholder's cash value will not decrease, even when the linked market index experiences negative growth. This floor is typically set at 0%, thereby guaranteeing that, at worst, the cash value will neither gain nor lose interest in a downturn. This mechanism mitigates the risk of market losses and assures that the principal thrives in a secure environment. During periods of market decline, the floor rate acts as a financial shield, enabling policyholders to focus on long-term growth without the immediate anxiety of losing built-up value.

Interest Crediting Mechanisms: Participation and Cap Rates

IUL policies employ sophisticated interest crediting strategies to balance growth potential with protection. Two pivotal components in this equation are participation rates and cap rates.

Participation Rate: This rate dictates the extent to which the policy's cash value participates in the gains of the underlying market index. For instance, if the participation rate is set at 80% and the index grows by 10%, the policyholder's cash value would be credited with interest reflecting an 8% gain. This approach offers substantial growth potential, empowering policyholders to profit from bullish market conditions without the accompanying risks of direct investments.

Cap Rate: The cap rate places an upper limit on interest that can be credited to the policy's cash value. This is the trade-off for the downside protection provided by the floor rate. For example, if the cap rate is 12%, and the market index increases by 15%, the policyholder would receive the maximum allowable increase of 12% in cash value. The cap ensures that the insurer can maintain a balanced risk profile, sustaining the zero-loss guarantee during tumultuous periods while still allowing policyholders to benefit significantly when markets perform well.

Balancing Risk and Reward

The interplay of floor and cap rates, alongside participation rates, positions IUL policies uniquely in the investment landscape. They provide a symbiotic blend of risk management and growth potential that is difficult to match with other conventional investment options. By securing a minimum guaranteed rate while enabling capped exposure to market gains, IULs craft a compelling narrative for wealth accumulation without the fear of erosion during economic downturns.

Strategic Financial Security

In conclusion, IUL policies offer robust mechanisms for downside protection, deftly mitigating the risks associated with stock market investments. By linking cash value growth to market indexes and utilizing tools like the floor rate, cap rates, and participation rates, policyholders are assured that their principal investments remain protected. This architecture not only shields against market volatility but also facilitates growth during stable periods, offering a harmonized blend of security and prosperity. Such intelligent wealth-building strategies underscore the importance of IULs in providing financial security and peace of mind in a perpetually shifting economic environment.

Case Studies of IUL Performance During Past Market Downturns

In the complex and often unpredictable financial landscape, safeguarding one's principal investment is paramount, especially during significant market downturns. Indexed Universal Life (IUL) policies have emerged as a robust financial instrument offering protection and growth potential, even in challenging economic times. Let us delve into historical data and case studies to illustrate how IUL policies have performed during notable market downturns, including the 2008 financial crisis and the 2020 market crash instigated by the COVID-19 pandemic. By examining these periods, we can understand how IUL policies' protective features have helped maintain principal and provided a measure of security when other investment vehicles faltered.

The 2008 Financial Crisis: A Test for Resilience

The 2008 financial crisis, a period of unprecedented economic turmoil, saw the collapse of major financial institutions, a severe downturn in stock markets, and a global economic recession. During this challenging time, many investments experienced significant depreciations, and investors faced severe capital erosions. However, policyholders with IULs experienced a different narrative.

IUL policies are tied to market indexes, like the S&P 500, but feature a key distinction: a built-in floor, typically ensuring that policyholders will not endure negative returns, even if the market drops. During the 2008 downturn, while index funds and stocks plunged, those invested in IUL policies saw their principal protected. For instance, consider an individual with an IUL policy with a growth cap of 11% and a floor of 0%. If the market index plummeted by 40%, the policyholder would not lose any principal as the policy guarantees a floor, highlighting the protective bubble encapsulating the investment.

Post-crisis, as markets began to recover, IUL policies participated in the upswing—albeit within the cap limits. This balance ensures steady growth while maintaining principal safety. The stories shared by individuals who had been relying upon their IUL policies during this period showcase the power of risk management fused with growth potential—a combination many traditional investment vehicles lacked during the financial collapse.

The 2020 Market Crash: Navigating Uncertainty Amidst a Pandemic

The COVID-19 pandemic of 2020 brought another test to global economies, causing abrupt market crashes and a swiftly changing investment landscape. With volatility becoming the norm, the financial markets faced significant dips, creating unease among investors. The Dow Jones and S&P 500 experienced dramatic drops, triggering fears of widespread capital loss. However, this was another proving ground for the effectiveness of Indexed Universal Life insurance.

What sets IUL policies apart during these downturns is their inherent ability to eschew the risk of negative returns. As the pandemic's effects unraveled, policyholders observed the zero-floor mechanism working seamlessly once again. A common scenario saw traditional investments deeply impacted, yet IUL contracts remained unfazed by the downturn due to their structure and guarantees.

Consider a real-world example: a policyholder whose portfolio was diversified across traditional stocks and an IUL. While the stock segment suffered depreciation, the IUL component not only shielded the principal but also positioned the individual to benefit from the subsequent recovery. Those protected holdings remained intact, allowing growth when market conditions stabilized.

Comparative Performance and Assurance

One must appreciate that the success of IULs during these market downturns stems from their unique design. Unlike direct stock investments, where volatility directly affects the value, IUL policies act as an insulated avenue. The safety net of a zero-percent floor brings unyielding security while removing the anxiety and loss potential other investment methods entail during economic recessions.

Furthermore, the tangible experiences shared by policyholders during these downturns provide assurance of IUL's efficacy as a strategic component of a diversified financial plan. While some investors faced the nerve-wracking experience of watching lifetime savings dwindle, IUL policyholders were grateful for their choice in seeking a stable, long-term growth mechanism that inherently includes downside protection.

In conclusion, case studies from these two significant market downturns, the 2008 financial crisis and the 2020 COVID-19 market crash—clearly indicate the resilience and protective strength of IUL policies. As an investment choice, they offer a compelling alternative for those prioritizing security and consistent growth even amidst financial turbulence. Through resilient protection and potent growth potential, IUL policies continue to underscore their importance in steadfast wealth-building strategies, providing a financially secure path for legacy-building and peace of mind.

Comparison with Traditional Investment Vehicles

When considering Indexed Universal Life (IUL) policies as a means of risk management during market downturns, it is crucial to understand how they compare with traditional investment vehicles like mutual funds, stocks, bonds, and 401(k) plans. Though each of these options serves a vital role in a diversified investment strategy, IUL policies offer unique advantages and protective features that warrant a closer look.

At the heart of an IUL policy is its dual nature, acting both as a life insurance product and an avenue for market-linked growth. Unlike traditional investments, IULs come with the promise of a death benefit, providing immediate financial security for beneficiaries. This aspect alone sets IULs apart, as traditional investments generally focus on accumulation without offering an inherent safeguard like life insurance.

A defining feature of IULs is the downside protection they offer. While mutual funds, stocks, and even 401(k) accounts are susceptible to market volatility, potentially leading to significant losses during economic downturns, IULs incorporate a floor rate—often set at 0% or 1%. This floor ensures that even in years of poor market performance, the policyholders' cash value does not decrease due to investment losses. Such a protective mechanism is absent in most traditional investment vehicles, where the principal is fully exposed to market dips.

Conversely, traditional investments do provide the opportunity for potentially higher returns during robust market periods. Mutual funds and stocks can often capitalize on market booms, and even 401(k) plans, with their diverse portfolio options, can benefit from significant appreciation over time. IULs, however, often come with caps on returns—limiting the amount of credit gained in periods of market growth. While floor rates guard against losses, these caps mean that policyholders might not fully capitalize on bull markets as they would with some traditional investments.

When comparing IULs to bonds, the conversation shifts to risk versus reward. Bonds are generally considered a safer investment compared to stocks, offering predictable payments, but their growth potential is relatively modest. IULs offer a more appealing balance by allowing participation in market gains—up to the policy's cap—without exposing the principal to loss, thereby blending growth opportunity with security in a way bonds cannot.

A look at 401(k) plans reveals further differences in risk management features. These employer-sponsored plans rely on investment in mutual funds, stocks, and bonds. While these plans can be advantageous, especially with employer matching contributions, they lack the inherent protection against market loss that IULs offer unless specifically allocated to stable income options. Additionally, the forced distribution of 401(k) funds upon reaching the age of 72 (in the form of Required Minimum Distributions) can expose retirees to unwanted tax implications, whereas IUL policy loans can be accessed on a tax-free basis, providing more flexibility in retirement planning.

However, it's worth noting that IULs come with their own set of trade-offs. The cost of insurance, administrative fees, and other associated charges can reduce the net returns for policyholders. On the flip side, these costs are part and parcel of the added protection and insurance benefits that traditional investments do not provide.

Ultimately, IULs offer a unique proposition: they blend life insurance with growth opportunities linked to market indexes, minus the direct exposure to market downturns. They ensure that even in tumultuous times, the policyholder can count on a floor that safeguards their cash value while still participating in market gains up to a specified cap. As with any financial product, it's essential to weigh these features against one's financial goals and risk tolerance. While IULs may not replace traditional investments outright, they present a complementary risk management tool in one's broader investment strategy. Balancing an IUL with conventional investment avenues could provide optimal growth potential while maintaining a safety net in times of economic uncertainty.

Strategic Planning for Principal Protection

When it comes to safeguarding your principal investment within an Indexed Universal Life (IUL) policy, strategic planning becomes your anchor during turbulent market conditions. While the allure of IULs often stems from their potential for tax-advantaged growth, equally pivotal is their ability to offer downside protection financial haven when markets falter. Below, we delve into actionable strategies for optimizing principal protection as an IUL policyholder, encompassing index selection, cap and floor rate adjustments, premium timing, and policy reviews.

1. Selecting the Right Index Options:

A cornerstone of principal protection within an IUL policy lies in selecting the appropriate index options that match your financial goals and risk tolerance. Typically, IUL policies are linked to major indexes like the S&P 500. These options allow you to capitalize on market gains while protecting against losses through strategically applied floors. It is crucial to evaluate the historical performance and volatility of different indexes while considering any fees or participation rate differences tied to them. Diversifying across multiple indexes can also mitigate risk and create a balanced approach that shields your principal.

2. Adjusting Cap and Floor Rates:

The cap rate, which limits the maximum return you can earn, and the floor rate, which protects you from losses, are vital components of an IUL policy. Understanding how these rates work and adjusting them according to your financial outlook can significantly affect principal protection. A higher cap allows for potential greater gains, but often this comes at the risk of a lower floor, which might compromise your protection during downturns. Conversely, opting for a policy with a robust floor rate ensures that your principal is safeguarded from market losses, albeit with potentially limited growth during bull markets.

3. Timing Premium Payments:

The timing of premium payments plays a substantial role in optimizing principal protection. By synchronizing your premium payment schedule with favorable market conditions, you allow your policy to take advantage of market upswings more effectively. When markets exhibit volatility or are on a downward trend, adjusting the timing of your payments can prevent exposure to immediate losses. Strategically planning premium payments during periods of probable economic growth allows you to maximize your credited interest while preserving your principal investment during less favorable times.

4. Policy Reviews and Economic Adjustments:

Regular policy reviews are an integral strategy for maintaining principal protection amidst evolving economic climates and personal financial objectives. Economic conditions are in constant flux, demanding that policyholders remain vigilant and proactive in their approach to policy management. Reviewing your IUL policy with a financial advisor periodically can ensure that you're not only aware of changes in cap or floor rates but also adjusting your strategy to echo shifts in the market or your own economic situation.

Life circumstances, such as changes in income, retirement timing, or health status, may also necessitate policy adjustments. By actively engaging in policy reviews, you prevent the erosion of your principal and maintain the flexibility to adapt your strategy as necessary. Such adaptive measures could involve reallocating index selections, modifying premium payment schedules, or adjusting loan and withdrawal plans to ensure continued protection and growth.

Strategically optimizing principal protection within an IUL policy demands a knowledgeable and proactive approach. From prudent index selection and savvy cap and floor adjustments to the precise timing of premium payments and diligent policy reviews, policyholders must exercise a comprehensive, agile strategy. This stance not only protects the principal amidst a sea of market volatility but also positions the policyholder to harness the true potential of IULs as a wealth-building tool. By embracing these strategies, you safeguard your financial foundations and fortify them against the unpredictable waves of economic downturns, thereby securing a stable and prosperous future.

Innovative Features and Riders that Enhance Principal Protection

In the ever-evolving landscape of financial planning, Indexed Universal Life (IUL) insurance has emerged as a formidable tool that not only offers growth potential through market-linked gains but also provides a robust mechanism for principal protection. A key element that distinguishes IUL from other financial instruments is the flexibility it offers through diverse riders and innovative features, catering to unique risk tolerances and financial objectives. These enhancements empower policyholders to secure their investments more comprehensively, especially during volatile market conditions.

One of the foremost features to consider is the **Guaranteed Minimum Withdrawal Benefit (GMWB) rider**. This feature ensures that policyholders can withdraw a specified amount from the policy's accumulated cash value, regardless of the policy's market-linked performance. In essence, the GMWB rider acts as a safety net, guaranteeing a minimum level of income, thereby providing confidence and peace of mind to investors whose primary concern is safeguarding their principal from market downturns.

Additionally, **Accidental Death Benefit (ADB) riders** serve to bolster the foundational protections of an IUL policy. The accidental death benefit rider provides an extra layer of coverage by increasing the death benefit if the insured passes away due to an accident. This enhancement is particularly appealing to individuals seeking to protect their families against unforeseen events, as it ensures that loved ones receive additional financial support in such tragic circumstances.

Another innovative option often available is the **Long-Term Care (LTC) rider**. This feature is vital when considering the escalating costs of healthcare and the potential financial burdens associated with long-term care. An LTC rider allows policyholders to access a portion of their death benefit to cover expenses related to long-term care needs. This adaptation ensures that even if the policyholder faces significant healthcare costs, their savings remain protected, and their loved ones are shielded from financial strain.

For those focused on accumulating cash value while maintaining policy stability, the **Option to Increase Death Benefit (OIDB) or increasing death benefit option** can be extremely beneficial. This rider allows policyholders to enhance the death benefit over time, in line with the policy's cash value growth. By aligning the death benefit with the accumulation of cash value, policyholders can protect against inflation and ensure their coverage remains adequate relative to their growing wealth.

Chronic Illness and Critical Illness riders further enrich the IUL policy's versatility. These riders offer acceleration of the policy's death benefit upon diagnosis of a qualifying chronic or critical illness, respectively. This means that policyholders have access to their death benefits when they're most vulnerable, providing financial relief without having to dip into core savings or principal investments. These features are particularly appealing to those looking to construct a comprehensive financial safety net that anticipates various life contingencies.

For those focused on premium flexibility, **Waiver of Premium for Disability** might prove indispensable. This rider ensures that if the policyholder becomes disabled and unable to earn an income, the insurance company will waive premium payments, keeping the policy active without financial strain. This protective measure is invaluable in maintaining the integrity of the policy during challenging personal circumstances without compromising the policyholder's financial commitment.

It's also important to explore the **Enhanced Cash Surrender Value Rider**, which amplifies liquidity during the early years of the policy. In times of financial uncertainty or emergency, this rider permits policyholders to access a higher cash surrender value than would typically be available. This liquidity feature allows for a strategic exit, ensuring that the policyholder isn't locked into a commitment if immediate access to funds becomes essential.

These riders and features aren't just about adding layers of protection; they are integral to tailoring the IUL policies to meet specific needs. Not every policyholder will require every feature, but having the option to include them creates a customizable safety net. This bespoke approach to policy design offers an unparalleled level of control over one's financial strategy.

In conclusion, the flexibility and adaptability of IUL policies through innovative features and riders allow policyholders to not only protect their principal but also enhance their financial journey according to personal goals and risk tolerances. As market dynamics continue to shift and personal circumstances evolve, these enhancements ensure that an IUL policy isn't just a static investment but a dynamic cornerstone of a holistic financial plan. For those striving to strike a balance between risk and security, understanding and leveraging these features is crucial in crafting a robust and resilient financial strategy for the future.

The Psychological and Financial Impact of Principal Protection on Policyholders

In the turbulent realm of financial markets, the psychological and financial well-being of investors is often as vital as the monetary gains they pursue. Indexed Universal Life (IUL) insurance policies offer a distinct advantage in the form of principal protection during market downturns. This powerful feature not only safeguards an individual's principal investment but also furnishes unparalleled psychological comfort and financial confidence to policyholders, fostering a steadfast environment conducive to long-term planning and stable financial behavior.

The Psychological Comfort of Principal Protection

At the core of human financial behavior lies a complex interplay of emotions—fear, greed, anxiety, and hope. These emotions are particularly pronounced during periods of economic volatility. When the market takes a downward turn, fear can lead to irrational decision-making and precipitate actions that compromise long-term financial goals. The principal protection inherent in IUL policies counteracts such emotionally driven decisions by offering a guaranteed safety net for the policyholder's initial investment.

This assurance of protection instills a deep sense of psychological comfort. Knowing that one's hard-earned capital is insulated from market fluctuations allows policyholders to remain calm and composed amid turmoil. Instead of reacting hastily to transient market conditions, individuals with IUL policies gain the confidence to adhere to their long-term financial strategies. This stability of mind is invaluable, as it can facilitate more prudent financial decisions that are in alignment with one's broader wealth-building objectives.

Financial Confidence and Long-Term Planning

The financial confidence engendered by IUL policies extends beyond mere preservation of capital. It serves as a catalyst for proactive financial planning. With the principal shielded from market losses, policyholders are emboldened to allocate resources towards achieving key life goals—such as funding a child's education, purchasing a home, or planning for retirement—without the continual anxiety over potential capital loss.

The downside protection ensures that even during the most uncertain periods, policyholders' plans remain on track. This offers a steadfast platform from which to navigate their financial journey, immune to the transient vicissitudes of market performance. Moreover, the consistent nature of policy cash value growth—tethered yet not fully exposed to market indexes—continues to compound, reinforcing the policyholder's wealth-building pursuits even amidst adverse conditions.

Insights from Financial Advisors and Policyholders

Financial advisors frequently emphasize the psychological merits of IUL policies to their clients, particularly those who exhibit risk-averse tendencies or are nearing retirement. Advisors highlight how the downside protection mechanism mitigates the impact of investment volatility on an individual's financial health, effectively creating a buffer that tempers portfolio risks.

From the perspective of policyholders, the peace of mind derived from knowing their principal investment is secure cannot be overstated. Many policyholders recount the relief and satisfaction experienced from maintaining their financial course without the disruptive influence of market swings. This sense of tranquility often translates into enhanced policyholder loyalty, as individuals who feel secure in their financial decisions are more inclined to continue investing in and advocating for IUL policies.

In times of market unpredictability, IUL policyholders report a pronounced reduction in financial stress. This reinforces the benefit of integrating principal protection into one's financial strategy, not merely as an investment tool, but as a robust risk management solution that fortifies overall financial security.

Principal protection, as offered by IUL policies, is more than just a shield against monetary loss. It is a cornerstone of financial and psychological resilience, empowering policyholders to embrace a strategic, long-term view of their financial landscape. The intrinsic security it provides fosters not only healthier financial habits but also nurtures a mindset geared towards sustained prosperity. In essence, the principal protection feature of IUL policies plays a crucial role in safeguarding not just an individual's financial assets but also their broader financial aspirations, contributing profoundly to a life of economic stability and confidence.

Chapter 5_Protecting Principal in Market Downturns

Definition and Mechanics of Downside Protection in IUL Policies

Within the realm of financial tools, Indexed Universal Life (IUL) insurance holds a unique position, offering an enticing blend of life insurance coverage and potential growth tied to market indexes. One of the most compelling features of IUL policies is their downside protection, crucial mechanism designed to shield the policyholder's principal investment during periods of market volatility. Understanding the definition and workings of downside protection in IUL policies is essential for appreciating the security and stability they provide in an unpredictable financial landscape.

Defining Downside Protection in IUL Policies

Downside protection in the context of IUL policies refers to the strategic design within these financial instruments that ensures the preservation of principal during market downturns. Unlike direct investments in the stock market or mutual funds, where investors are directly exposed to market fluctuations, IUL policies mitigate this risk by eliminating the possibility of negative returns. The cornerstone of this protection is the policy's floor—a predetermined minimum return rate, often guaranteed at 0% or 1%, below which the policyholder's cash value will not decrease due to poor market performance. This means that even in a year when the linked index, such as the S&P 500, suffers significant losses, the policyholder's principal remains intact, and no negative returns are experienced.

Mechanics of Downside Protection

The mechanics of downside protection in IUL policies revolve around the intricate interplay between the policy's index accounts, caps, participation rates, and floors. Here's how these elements work together to foster security during market downtrends:

1. Index Accounts and Crediting Strategies:

IUL policies accumulate cash value based on the performance of one or more selected market indexes. These indexes typically include major benchmarks like the S&P 500. The policyholder's cash value growth is tied to the index's performance, yet it does not involve direct investment in the stock market. As such, the actual funds are not susceptible to the day-to-day fluctuations of stock prices. Instead, the cash value's growth is credited based on pre-defined strategies aligned with the index's performance, which include predetermined caps and participation rates.

2. Caps and Participation Rates:

The cap represents the maximum interest rate that can be credited to the policyholder's account in a given period, usually annually. For example, if the cap is set at 10% and the linked index achieves a return of 15%, the credited interest will not exceed 10%. Conversely, the participation rate determines the percentage of the index's gain that will be credited to the policy. A participation rate of 80%, for instance, means the cash value will grow by 80% of the index's total gain, subject to the cap. These constraints serve as a balancing mechanism, allowing policyholders to enjoy the upside potential of market-linked growth while securing their investment against downturns.

3. Floor and Principal Security:

The floor ensures that the policyholder's cash value does not decrease due to index losses. For instance, with a 0% floor, if the market index experiences a negative return, the policyholder's account will not be debited for that loss. This protective measure is the hallmark of downside protection in IUL policies, reinforcing the policyholder's confidence that their invested principal will remain unscathed, regardless of market turbulence.

4. Cost of Insurance and Administrative Charges:

While downside protection shields the policyholder from market volatility, it's essential to note that regular cost of insurance (COI) and administrative charges continue to apply. These costs are necessary for maintaining the policy and are deducted from the cash value or premium payments. However, they do not influence the safety net of downside protection that guards against market losses.

Benefits of Downside Protection

The benefits of downside protection in IUL policies extend beyond principal security, promoting a stable growth environment for long-term financial planning. Policyholders can pursue potential upside gains without the anxiety associated with market dips, facilitating strategic financial goal setting such as retirement planning and legacy building. Additionally, during periods of economic uncertainty, the ability to stabilize investments without exposing the principal to risk is a strategic advantage that sets IUL policies apart as a robust financial tool.

In conclusion, the definition and mechanics of downside protection within IUL policies highlight a sophisticated structure engineered to navigate market adversities. This protection not only secures the principal but also empowers policyholders to engage with growth opportunities confidently, knowing that their investment is shielded from the inevitable ebbs and flows of financial markets.

Real-World Examples of Principal Preservation During Recessions

Market downturns and recessions, those dreaded yet inevitable phases in the economic cycle, can erode investment portfolios and upset even the most meticulously crafted financial plans. However, Indexed Universal Life (IUL) policies have stood as stalwart defenders of principal during such financial storms. By examining real-world scenarios, we can see how policyholders have effectively utilized IUL insurance to preserve their principal investment during challenging economic times.

The 2008 Financial Crisis

The 2008 financial crisis, often dubbed the Great Recession, was a testament to the tumultuous nature of financial markets. Amid collapsing banks and plummeting stock values, many investors watched helplessly as their portfolios diminished. However, holders of IUL policies experienced a starkly different scenario.

IULs feature a unique design where the cash value is linked to a market index like the S&P 500 but is safeguarded by a "floor." This floor, often set at 0%, ensures that no matter how poorly the market performs, the cash value of the policy does not decrease due to market performance. During the 2008 crisis, while many equity investments suffered losses upwards of 40%, IUL policies preserved the principal, as these negatives were mitigated to zero where policyholders neither lost value nor gained, a stark contrast to the widespread market-induced losses seen elsewhere.

The COVID-19 Pandemic

The onset of the COVID-19 pandemic in early 2020 ushered in a period of unprecedented volatility and uncertainty. Markets reacted sharply, with dramatic drops occurring seemingly overnight. Many traditional investment vehicles, vulnerable to such market shocks, faltered. IUL policyholders, however, continued to experience the resilience of their investment strategy.

One notable example involved family planning for their child's college education. Their cash-value accumulation within the IUL policy was shielded from the market's downside through the policy's structural guarantee. As the crisis unfolded, they maintained their policy's value and continued to see potential growth in subsequent market recovery periods without the worry of having to recoup from earlier losses. This stability offered peace of mind and ensured that plans for major financial goals remained unchanged despite external economic upheaval.

The Robustness of IUL in Diverse Economic Conditions

IUL policies have been employed by both individuals and businesses as a component of comprehensive financial strategies. During the dot-com bubble of the late 1990s and early 2000s, many tech stocks, and equities dependent on them, faced significant downsizing. On the other hand, policyholders of IULs saw their investments remain consistent.

Consider the case of a mid-sized business utilizing an IUL policy for key person insurance. As the external markets took nosedives, their IUL policy acted almost like a financial buoy—keeping crucial insurance coverage intact and allowing the company to navigate through economic distress without the need for abrupt changes in strategy or withdrawal of funds for financial stability.

Additionally, policyholders benefiting from the tax-advantaged aspect of IUL, during periods of economic strain, found the ability to loan against the cash value to meet liquidity needs without incurring tax penalties. This multifaceted approach to financial security provided both immediate and long-term advantages, a benefit underscore visible in various economic scenarios.

Lessons From Real-World IUL Experiences

The common thread identified in these real-world examples is clear: IUL policies offer a reliable mechanism for principal preservation when markets falter. The zero-loss floor, combined with the growth potential tied to positive market performance, reinforces the IUL's role as a cornerstone in diversifying a portfolio against financial downturns.

This capability does not eliminate market risk entirely but surrogates it with strategic insulation that can be enhanced when integrated with a broader financial strategy. Individuals can further bolster their path to financial security by analyzing these examples and understanding how Indexed Universal Life insurance can serve as a robust tool, ensuring protection against market downturns while also advancing wealth-building opportunities.

Overall, these real-world cases illuminate the multifaceted value of IUL policies as a prudent choice for those prioritizing principal preservation amid market volatility. This approach empowers individuals and businesses alike to look beyond immediate market fluctuations, maintaining a steady course toward long-term financial objectives.

Comparison of IUL with Traditional Safe Havens

In times of economic uncertainty, investors often seek refuge in financial instruments that promise capital preservation above all else. Historically, traditional safe havens like bonds, precious metals, and savings accounts have been the go-to options for risk-averse investors. However, in recent years, Indexed Universal Life (IUL) insurance policies have emerged as a compelling alternative. While each of these options has its strengths and weaknesses, IUL policies offer a unique combination of protection, growth potential, and flexibility that sets them apart.

Bonds: Stability with Limited Growth

Bonds, particularly those issued by government entities and highly rated corporations, are classic staples in the safe haven portfolio. They are seen as relatively secure since they come with the promise of principal repayment upon maturity, alongside periodic interest payments. However, the main drawback of bonds is their susceptibility to interest rate risks. When interest rates rise, existing bonds with lower coupons become less attractive, leading to potential declines in market value. Inflation risk is another concern, as it erodes the purchasing power of the fixed interest payments over time.

IUL policies, in contrast, are not directly subject to interest rate fluctuations or inflation in the same way. While the crediting strategies within IUL are tied to market indices such as the S&P 500, these policies offer downside protection through structured caps and participation rates, meaning the cash value may not decrease even when markets perform poorly. This approach can potentially yield higher returns over the long term compared to bonds, without the interest rate risk typically associated with bond investments.

Precious Metals: A Tangible Yet Volatile Safe Haven

Precious metals like gold and silver have traditionally been viewed as hedges against economic turbulence and currency devaluation. Their allure stems from their intrinsic value and historical perception as stores of wealth. However, precious metals carry their own set of challenges. Their market prices can be highly volatile, influenced by global economic conditions, currency fluctuations, and demand-supply dynamics. Moreover, physical ownership of metals incurs storage and insurance costs, adding to the overall investment consideration.

IUL policies, though devoid of physical ownership allure, present a more stable and predictable alternative. Unlike precious metals, which offer no dividends or interest, an IUL policy provides the potential to participate in market gains, with credited interest linked to the performance of chosen indices while guaranteeing protection from negative returns.

Savings Accounts: Safety at the Cost of Growth

Savings accounts in banks represent the epitome of safety guaranteed by federal insurance up to a certain limit in many countries. This assurance of principal preservation is unmatched but comes at a significant cost:

virtually nonexistent growth. Given today's low-interest rate environment, savings account returns often fail to keep pace with inflation, resulting in real-value erosion over time.

IUL policies, though not possessing the absolute safety of federally-insured deposits, offer significant advantages in growth potential. The interest credited to an IUL's cash value, based on index performance, often surpasses the minimal yield provided by savings accounts. Furthermore, the tax advantages inherent in the growth of an IUL policy's cash value make it a more potent tool for long-term wealth accumulation compared to the stagnant returns in traditional savings vehicles.

Flexibility and Additional Benefits of IUL

Beyond the core component of principal protection and growth potential, IUL policies offer benefits that traditional safe havens do not. One such benefit is flexibility. Policyholders can modify premium payments and death benefits over time, potentially adapting to changing financial circumstances. Additionally, IUL policies provide the opportunity to access cash value through policy loans and withdrawals, offering liquidity options that can be utilized without the tax implications of liquidating other investment assets.

Furthermore, the death benefit aspect of IUL policies is nothing to be underrated. It offers an immediate and tax-free legacy to beneficiaries, ensuring wealth transfer efficiency that traditional safe haven investments cannot replicate.

Differentiated Protection and Growth

In totality, while traditional safe havens like bonds, precious metals, and savings accounts each have their respective roles in protecting principal during market downturns, Indexed Universal Life policies present a differentiated and versatile alternative. With their unique blend of protection against market losses, growth potential linked to market indices, and added advantages such as tax efficiency, adjustable features, and wealth transfer capabilities, IUL policies represent a formidable option for those seeking to safeguard and grow their wealth through uncertain economic climates. As investment paradigms evolve, IUL policies continue to carve out a niche as an innovative blend of insurance and investment, redefining what it means to protect principal in the modern financial landscape.

IUL Versus Other Life Insurance Products During Downturns

In the dynamic world of life insurance, where market stability can often appear elusive,

Indexed Universal Life (IUL) insurance policies emerge as a robust contender offering unparalleled security during economic downturns. To the discerning policyholder seeking not just protection but also capital preservation, understanding how IULs interweave the twin premises of investment growth and downside protection is crucial. In this segment, we shall dissect the comparative advantages of IULs over other life insurance products such as Whole Life Insurance, Variable Universal Life (VUL), and Universal Life Insurance (UL) during market downturns.

At its core, an Indexed Universal Life policy is designed to provide a unique combination of life insurance protection and investment opportunity. IULs are linked to a stock market index, like the S&P 500, enabling the cash value component of the policy to grow as the market performs well. The salient feature that sets IULs apart is their innate structure to prevent losses during market downturns. This is achieved through the provision of a floor, ensuring that the returns never go negative, even when the associated index posts a loss. Unlike other market-linked investments where downturns can severely impact invested capital, the IUL's floor mechanism provides peace of mind to policyholders that their principal is safeguarded.

Comparatively, Whole Life Insurance offers a more predictable path, providing guaranteed cash value growth and death benefits. However, during downturns, the growth in cash value is solely reliant on the dividends declared by the insurance company, which might not always be reflective of broader market conditions. While these dividends are generally stable, they do not offer the same growth potential found in IULs during bull markets. Thus, Whole Life Insurance, while secure, lacks the opportunity for enhanced growth during economic recoveries that IULs can capitalize on.

Variable Universal Life Insurance, or VUL, provides investment choices among various sub-accounts that resemble mutual funds. While this allows policyholders to tailor their investment strategies according to risk appetites, it also exposes them to direct market risks. In periods of economic contraction, the cash value of a VUL can decrease significantly, reflecting the downturns in the selected investments. This lack of a stabilizing feature similar to the IUL's floor means that VUL policyholders might face diminished value at precisely the moments they seek reassurance and preservation of assets.

Universal Life Insurance (UL), by contrast, offers flexibility in premium payments and the potential to build cash value, albeit at subdued rates compared to IULs. During market downturns, a traditional UL policy might provide stability due to its fixed nature. However, since the cash value accrual is commonly tied to a prevailing interest rate, which might be adversely impacted by economic stagnation, policyholders often find their UL growth rates less competitive in fluctuating economic climates.

One of the profound advantages of IUL policies during downturns is the strategic harnessing of downside protection matched with upside potential. IULs employ a cap rate in addition to the floor, enabling growth within defined parameters. While this approach means that the policyholder might not capture the absolute highest market gains, it effectively enforces a protective band within which the cash value can securely grow or remain secured.

Moreover, the intrinsic flexibility within IULs allows for adaptation according to market conditions. Policyholders can adjust premium payments and the amount of coverage according to life situations and changing economic climates, ensuring a personalized alignment with financial goals. This flexibility, tethered with the innovative growth potential and stabilizing features of IULs, creates a conducive environment for long-term financial planning even as external economic forces fluctuate.

In conclusion, when navigating the unsteady waters of economic downturns, Indexed Universal Life Insurance policies emerge as a sophisticated option offering balanced protection and growth. With the assurance that their principal is guarded from market losses, policyholders can maintain focus on long-term financial objectives with an IUL policy. While alternative life insurance products—such as Whole Life, VUL, and UL—each present unique benefits, none combine the shielding floor and growth-enabling capabilities quite like the IUL. Whether for the security-seeking individual or the investment-savvy policyholder, IULs hold a distinct advantage during the turbulent times, making them a compelling choice for financial security and growth.

Strategic Policy Management for Enhancing Downside Protection

When considering financial instruments designed to mitigate risks during market downturns, few options offer the robust protective features of an Indexed Universal Life (IUL) policy. At its core, an IUL policy is a dynamic financial tool that balances growth potential with strategic risk management. This blend is particularly vital during adverse economic climates when protecting one's principal investment becomes paramount. To harness the full potential of an IUL policy's downside protection, one must delve into strategic policy management, which involves understanding the policy's inherent mechanisms, optimizing its features, and adapting to changing conditions.

One of the key features of an IUL policy is its participation in market index performance without direct investment into the market itself. This unique structure provides a form of downside protection inherently baked into the policy's design. During market downturns, a well-managed IUL policy shields policyholders from loss of principal due to its zero-floor feature. In essence, while policyholders can benefit from potential market gains through the linking of their cash value to an index like the S&P 500, they do not suffer losses when the index declines. This is because IUL policies guarantee a minimum credited interest rate, ensuring that even in a severe market downturn, the policy's cash value and death benefit remain secure.

Strategic management of an IUL policy begins with selecting a product that aligns with one's risk tolerance, financial goals, and anticipated market conditions. Policyholders must analyze and choose among various index crediting strategies offered. Popular ones include the annual point-to-point method and the monthly sum crediting strategy. Each has its unique way of calculating interest credits based on market performance. By understanding these strategies, policyholders can tailor their policy to optimize for both potential returns and protection.

Furthermore, policyholders should evaluate the index account options and their associated participation rates and caps. Participation rates determine the percentage of the index's gain that is credited to the policy, while caps impose an upper limit on the earnings one can receive from index-linked growth. Adjusting these variables in alignment with market expectations and personal financial objectives forms the crux of strategic policy management. During periods of high market volatility or expected downturns, opting for a strategy with a higher floor and lower cap can prioritize preservation overgrowth, minimizing risk exposure.

Regularly reviewing and adjusting one's policy allocation is another crucial element of strategic policy management. As market conditions evolve and personal circumstances change, periodic reassessment of the policy ensures that it continues to meet financial goals effectively. This may involve shifting allocations between fixed and indexed accounts or opting for different index strategies based on prevailing market forecasts and economic analyses.

Moreover, leveraging policy riders can further enhance downside protection. For instance, adding a no-lapse guarantee rider ensures that the policy remains in force regardless of market conditions, provided the specified premiums are paid. This type of rider can be invaluable during economic downturns when maintaining the policy's stability and future benefits becomes a priority.

Policyholders should also engage in proactive premium management. During challenging economic times, the flexibility to adjust premium payments can be vital. IUL policies often allow for premium adjustments and the use of accumulated cash value to cover premiums without lapsing the policy. This flexibility ensures that financial strain does not compromise the longevity or efficacy of the policy.

Lastly, it's essential to work closely with a financial advisor who understands the complexities of IUL policies. An experienced advisor can aid in fine-tuning the policy structure and make informed suggestions about adjusting index strategies, participation rates, and policy riders based on comprehensive market analyses and individual financial circumstances.

In conclusion, while the built-in protective mechanisms of an IUL policy inherently offer significant downside protection during market downturns, these benefits are maximized through strategic policy management. By understanding and adeptly navigating the sophisticated architecture of IUL policies, policyholders can secure their principal investment, safeguard their financial future, and potentially benefit from market growth—all while maintaining a stable and secure financial cushion in the face of economic adversity. This proactive and informed approach sets IUL policies apart from many other investment options, affirming their role as a cornerstone in a diversified and resilient financial strategy.

Future Outlook and the Evolving Role of IUL in Risk Management

As we peer into the future of financial planning and risk management, one thing becomes abundantly clear: Indexed Universal Life (IUL) insurance is increasingly poised to play a pivotal role. The landscape of financial strategies and risk management tools is always in flux, shaped by economic shifts, regulatory changes, and technological advancements. IUL policies, with their unique blend of life insurance and investment potential, often stand out as a flexible, multifaceted solution for individuals seeking to safeguard their financial futures.

The Growing Need for Downside Protection

In an ever-evolving economic environment, market volatility seems almost constant. Frequent fluctuations create anxiety around preserving capital—a concern at the forefront for many investors, particularly those nearing retirement. In this context, the appeal of IUL policies is significant. With their ability to offer upside potential linked to market indices like the S&P 500, while simultaneously providing guarantees against market downturns through a zero percent floor, IULs are uniquely positioned. This assurance that policyholders will not lose principal due to market declines creates a robust safety net, drawing a growing interest in IULs as a dependable risk management tool.

Simultaneously, as more individuals assume responsibility for their financial planning, thanks in part to the continuous decline of employer-managed pension plans, the self-directed nature of IUL policies is increasingly attractive. They offer the dual advantages of mitigating market risk while providing policyholders with autonomy over their financial growth strategies.

Technological Innovations and IUL Policy Enhancements

The future of IUL also revolves around technological advancements shaping how these products are designed, managed, and sold.

Insurtech, a burgeoning field within financial technology, is beginning to revolutionize the insurance industry. With advancements such as artificial intelligence and big data analytics, insurance providers are achieving unprecedented levels of personalization in policy development. This means that consumers can expect more tailored IUL products that align perfectly with their financial goals and risk tolerance levels.

Additionally, technological innovations in financial management tools enable better real-time monitoring and management of IUL policies. These advancements provide policyholders with the detailed insights necessary to make informed decisions, potentially increasing the efficiency with which they can navigate economic downturns.

Regulatory Developments and Their Impact

Regulatory frameworks surrounding life insurance and investment products are always in flux, impacted by broader economic and political shifts. IUL policies, too, are subject to this influence. Governments across the globe are continuously adapting regulations to reflect the changing financial landscape and protect consumers. Navigating these changes requires awareness and adaptability from both policyholders and insurers, as staying compliant ensures that the benefits of IUL policies are fully realized.

Looking ahead, increased regulatory focus on transparency and consumer protection could streamline product offerings and lead to further innovations designed to enhance the clarity and attractiveness of IUL policies as financial instruments for risk management.

A Shift Towards Holistic Financial Planning

As financial consumers become savvier and better informed, the demand for holistic financial planning solutions increases. IUL policies are in a prime position to fulfill this need due to their multifarious nature—integrating life insurance coverage, investment growth potential, and downside protection all within a single financial product. The role of IUL policies in risk management is likely to continue evolving, adapting to the shifting paradigms of personal finance and wealth management.

Moreover, as financial literacy improves and individuals seek integrated solutions that address multiple financial objectives—such as wealth accumulation, retirement planning, and legacy planning—IULs are uniquely equipped to satisfy these needs. Their ability to blend tax advantages, investment potential, and protection seamlessly into one plan makes them viable contenders in future-focused financial strategies.

The Indexed Universal Life insurance sector holds significant promise as part of the future risk management toolkit. As economic conditions and technological landscapes evolve, IUL policies are likely to play an integral role in securing financial peace of mind. By providing robust downside protection while allowing for growth potential, seamlessly incorporating technological advancements, and adapting to regulatory changes, IUL policies enhance their appeal as a sustainable, adaptable component in risk management and financial planning. This bodes well for current and future policyholders in their quest for financial security in an unpredictable world.

Chapter 6 Achieving Financial Milestones

Overview of Major Financial Goals and the Role of IUL

Financial goals vary across different stages of life. Whether it's setting aside funds for a comfortable retirement, ensuring your children receive the best education possible, or safeguarding against potential future hardships, the goals often entail making deliberate financial choices. Indexed Universal Life (IUL) insurance stands as a versatile tool designed to assist in funding these paramount life objectives. With its intrinsic benefits of both life insurance protection and dynamic cash value growth, an IUL policy encompasses the necessary components to bolster the achievement of major financial goals.

Retirement Planning: A primary financial goal for most individuals is preparing for retirement. With life expectancies increasing, building a substantial retirement fund has become more critical than ever. IUL policies contribute to this goal by offering the potential for tax-deferred growth of the policy's cash value. Unlike other traditional retirement vehicles, such as 401(k)s or IRAs, which are often limited by annual contribution caps and taxed upon withdrawal, the cash value within an IUL grows tax-deferred and can be accessed tax-free when structured correctly. This unique attribute provides policyholders with a stream of tax-advantaged income during their retirement years, enabling them to maintain their lifestyle and cover ongoing expenses without the burden of heavy taxation.

Funding Education Expenses: Next to retirement, funding education for children or grandchildren frequently surfaces as a significant financial objective. The escalating costs of higher education are a concern for many. An IUL policy can be strategically employed to build cash value that may be utilized for educational expenses, offering flexibility and a variety of funding options. Unlike traditional savings plans like 529 College Savings Plans, an IUL does not restrict the use of funds solely to educational purposes, providing policyholders with the liberty to reallocate funds as life circumstances evolve. Moreover, when the cash value from an IUL is accessed as a policy loan or withdrawal, it may not be counted as income on the Free Application for Federal Student Aid (FAFSA), potentially allowing the student to qualify for more financial aid.

Protecting Against the Unexpected: Life is unpredictable, and unforeseen events such as accidents, health issues, or loss of employment can impose serious financial strain. Building a substantial emergency fund is a vital financial objective for security against such occurrences. Here, IUL plays a vital role by offering the option to tap into the policy's cash value. Loans or withdrawals from IUL can provide immediate liquidity in times of crisis, without incurring any early withdrawal penalties that typically accompany traditional investment accounts.

Legacy Planning: A long-term financial goal for many is to leave a meaningful legacy. An IUL policy is inherently designed to facilitate this through its death benefit, which is paid out tax-free to beneficiaries. This feature ensures that heirs receive a substantial financial sum, allowing policyholders to leave behind a legacy reflective of their values and careful planning. Advanced IUL strategies can further enhance this benefit, offering methods to maximize the tax-free sum passed on, effectively contributing to multi-generational wealth transfer.

Tax Planning and Diversification: In the realm of tax planning, IUL plays a strategic role by offering tax diversification. This multidimensional financial tool transcends the conventional approach of merely minimizing current tax liabilities. Instead, it provides a proactive method for mitigating future tax impacts. By integrating an IUL into a diversified financial plan, policyholders can balance against taxable income sources, optimizing their overall tax strategy across both pre- and post-retirement phases.

Conclusion: IUL serves as a multifaceted instrument that aligns seamlessly with various major financial goals. Whether it's accumulating a sizeable retirement fund, covering the escalating costs of education, providing for unforeseen emergencies, ensuring a tax-efficient transfer of wealth, or facilitating meticulous tax planning, this policy type offers a robust platform to build and protect wealth. Its adaptability, tax advantages, and growth potential make IUL a pivotal asset in any comprehensive financial strategy. Ultimately, choosing to incorporate IUL policies enables individuals and families to not only aspire to meet their financial goals but to achieve them with a higher degree of certainty and foresight.

Retirement Planning Using IUL

When charting the course towards a financially secure retirement, the landscape of options can be overwhelming. Various investment vehicles promise to safeguard your future, yet they often fall short when it comes to a blend of growth potential, tax advantages, and risk mitigation. **Enter Indexed Universal Life (IUL) insurance** — a versatile financial instrument that offers a balanced solution through its unique structure, designed to cater to both growth and preservation of your assets.

Understanding IULs in the Context of Retirement

Before diving deeper into the specifics of using IULs for retirement, it's crucial to grasp the structure of these policies. At its core, an IUL policy is a permanent life insurance product with a cash value component that grows based on a specific stock market index, like the S&P 500. The key attraction for retirement planning lies in the tax-deferred growth of the cash value and the ability to access this tax-free growth through policy loans and withdrawals.

Mitigating Market Risks

One of the biggest concerns for retirees relying on traditional investment avenues is market volatility. Sharp market downturns can wreak havoc on portfolios, potentially delaying retirement or forcing undesirable lifestyle changes. IULs offer a protective buffer through their structure, providing guaranteed minimum interest rates which protect your cash value from negative market years. While your cash value can grow when indexes perform well, you're safeguarded from losses when they falter. It's this "floor" feature that allows retirees to have a peace of mind, knowing their principal investment is shielded from the market's most vicious downturns.

Tax-efficient Withdrawals

Retirement income stability hinges largely on tax-efficient strategies. With IULs, you have the advantage of accessing your policy's accumulated values through tax-free loans and withdrawals. This mechanism can serve as a powerful supplement to other retirement income sources, ensuring that you don't inadvertently jump into a higher tax bracket due to taxable distributions, a common problem with traditional retirement accounts like 401(k)s or IRAs.

Flexibility in Retirement Planning

Beyond tax and risk considerations, IULs offer unparalleled flexibility which is often absent in other retirement planning tools. For instance, while IRAs and 401(k)s have contribution limits and required minimum distributions (RMDs) that start at a certain age, IULs offer no such constraints. You're in control of your contributions and can tailor your premium payments around your financial situation and objectives. During retirement, you decide when and how much to withdraw, aligning with your actual needs and changing circumstances.

Funding Long-term Goals with Confidence

A robust retirement plan also accounts for unexpected expenses, such as healthcare costs or long-term care needs. IULs can be crafted with riders that provide living benefits, allowing you the option to access death benefits for specific long-term care expenses or critical illness costs without encroaching into your asset pool significantly. It's this incorporation of life contingencies that makes IULs exceedingly advantageous for comprehensive retirement strategies.

Legacy Planning and Retirement

Retirement is also a time to think about legacy planning, ensuring that loved ones are financially secure upon your passing. The death benefit intrinsic to all IUL policies supports this goal, providing heirs with tax-free proceeds. Moreover, because IULs are inherently within the domain of life insurance, the transfer of wealth is often more efficient than other asset transfer methods, bypassing probate and potentially reducing estate taxes.

The Drawbacks

While IULs present a compelling case for retirement planning, they are not without their drawbacks. It's imperative to understand the potential fees associated with IUL, which can include cost of insurance charges, administrative fees, and surrender charges for early withdrawal or policy lapses. Only by ensuring these are balanced against your financial objectives and lifespan expectations, can you fully leverage an IUL's potential for your retirement plan.

An Indexed Universal Life insurance policy can be a dynamic cornerstone in a well-rounded retirement plan. Its capabilities to shield against market losses, deliver tax-efficient withdrawals, and provide a flexible framework for both asset growth and legacy protection make it an attractive option worth considering for individuals intent on proactive and strategic retirement planning. However, as with all financial products, due diligence, and alignment with personal financial goals are paramount to realizing its full benefits.

Funding Education through IUL

In the intricate realm of financial planning, one enduring challenge stands out prominently—the quest to fund educational pursuits without succumbing to crippling debt. As education costs continue to ascend, parents and grandparents diligently seek strategies that not only accumulate value over time but also provide flexibility and tax advantages. Enter Indexed Universal Life (IUL) insurance—a surprisingly versatile tool in the financial arsenal, offering a distinctive pathway to funding education with an array of compelling benefits.

An IUL policy is ingeniously designed to build cash value by linking to market indexes such as the S&P 500 while simultaneously providing a death benefit. This dynamic structure makes IUL an appealing alternative to traditional education savings plans like 529 plans or Coverdell Education Savings Accounts. Although those may offer tax advantages, they come with restrictions on how and when the funds can be used, and often they expose the savings to market risk. In contrast, IUL policies offer a strategic blend of growth potential, downside protection, and tax-deferred accumulation.

One of the key attractions of using an IUL for funding education is the inherent flexibility it provides. Unlike 529 plans, which must be used for qualified educational expenses to enjoy tax benefits, the cash value in an IUL policy can be used for any purpose—be it tuition fees, accommodation, books, or even living expenses. Additionally, if the child's educational pursuits change—say, they decide to start a business or travel the world instead of going to college—the funds can be repurposed without penalty, a freedom not extended by most dedicated educational savings plans.

Let's delve deeper into the mechanisms that make IULs particularly adept at funding education. The cash value within an IUL policy grows tax-deferred, meaning that policyholders will not have to pay taxes on earnings as they accumulate. This can substantially increase the growth potential over time compared to taxable savings accounts. When it comes time to access the funds for educational expenses, one can utilize policy loans, which come with the benefit of being tax-free, assuming the policy remains in force. This access not only provides liquidity but also avoids potential early withdrawal penalties and tax hits that might accompany other saving strategies.

Moreover, the structured capability of IUL to offer downside protection ensures that the cash value in the policy won't diminish due to negative index performance—a critical feature, especially when the funds are earmarked for something as vital as education. This safeguard makes it a more serene harbor in turbulent financial times compared to direct stock market investments.

Beyond these advantages, IULs also allow for continued growth of cash value even when funds are drawn for education, thanks to the way most policies credit interest based on the original account value, not the diminished figure after loans. This is akin to having a residence that appreciates in value despite tapping into its equity—a beneficial feature for those looking to maximize both current benefits for education funding and the growth of their long-term financial portfolio.

Furthermore, the added peace of mind with IUL policies comes from the knowledge that the death benefit remains intact. In the unfortunate scenario that the policyholder passes away while the child is still pursuing education, the death benefit can provide not only the means to continue education uninterrupted but also financial protection for other facets of the beneficiary's life.

Understanding the implications and structuring the most effective use of an IUL policy can be complex, and therefore it requires diligent consideration and expertise. It becomes crucial to tailor an IUL to fit personal financial circumstances and educational aspirations, keeping in tune with premium commitments and desired outcomes. Nevertheless, by strategically utilizing the multifaceted benefits of IUL policies, families can indeed secure a versatile and robust method to meet the financial demands of higher education.

It's important to note that while IUL offers numerous advantages, it should be integrated thoughtfully into a comprehensive financial plan. Prospective policyholders should engage with financial advisors who possess profound expertise in insurance products to navigate the nuances of IUL policies and effectively align them with their educational savings goals. This diligent planning and informed decision-making are essential to unlocking the full potential of IULs as an educational funding vehicle, ensuring a future where academic dreams can be pursued without the shadow of financial strain.

IUL as an Emergency Fund

In the intricate tapestry of financial planning, strategically utilizing certain instruments for multiple purposes can greatly enhance one's financial resilience. Indexed Universal Life (IUL) insurance policies, typically lauded for their tax-advantaged wealth-building opportunities, can also serve as a reliable emergency fund. The unique structure and advantages of IUL make it not only a vehicle for long-term growth but also a readily accessible safety net in times of financial need. In this subpoint, we'll explore how IUL policies can function as an effective emergency fund, providing liquidity, preserving capital, and maintaining a growth trajectory even when life's unpredictable turns require immediate financial action.

Liquidity and Accessibility

One of the foremost advantages of IUL policies is their inherent liquidity, which is a crucial characteristic for any asset intended to serve as an emergency fund. The cash value component of an IUL policy is accessible to the policyholder, typically through policy loans or withdrawals. Such accessibility means that in the event of an unforeseen expense—whether it be a medical emergency, sudden job loss, or urgent home repairs, the policyholder can quickly obtain the necessary funds without needing to undergo the arduous process of applying for a traditional loan or liquidating other investments like stocks or real estate, which may involve penalties or unfavorable market conditions.

Policy loans allow the policyholder to borrow against the cash value of their IUL policy without triggering a taxable event. This is profoundly significant as it ensures liquidity while protecting the policyholder from immediate tax consequences, which is often a concern when accessing other forms of retirement savings. Moreover, since the policyholder is essentially borrowing from themselves, these loans typically come with flexible repayment terms. This flexibility provides a significant psychological and financial buffer during times of distress, as the immediate focus can remain on handling the emergency rather than fulfilling loan obligations.

Capital Preservation

Indexed Universal Life insurance policies also offer a degree of capital preservation that is uncommon in many other emergency fund alternatives. Unlike mutual funds or stocks, which are susceptible to market volatility and can result in losses if redemptions coincide with a market downturn, IUL policies typically come with a downside protection feature. This means that while the cash value of the policy is linked to index performance such as the S&P 500—it is simultaneously insulated from direct market losses. In scenarios where there's a market decline, the cash value does not decrease; instead, it may simply remain flat, ensuring that the principal is safeguarded.

This protection ensures that when emergencies occur, and funds are needed, the value accessed from the IUL policy is not diminished by adverse market conditions. It forms a stable financial base from which policyholders can draw resources with the confidence that their future financial goals remain unscathed.

Continued Growth Potential

Beyond liquidity and protection, the cash value inside an IUL policy continues to benefit from potential growth, even as funds are withdrawn or borrowed against it. This stems from the fact that the loan taken from the policy's cash value does not alter the amount credited for growth purposes; rather, the policyholder effectively borrows against the death benefit of the policy.

In a practical sense, this means that while you have accessed cash to address an emergency, your policy continues to earn based on the full cash value as it is linked to index performance. Consequently, an IUL policy ensures that both your immediate financial needs and long-term wealth accumulation potential are simultaneously addressed. This dual functionality greatly surpasses what is available through other emergency fund solutions, like savings accounts, which offer limited or no growth potential.

A Strategic Component of a Holistic Plan

Integrating IUL as an emergency fund within your broader financial strategy provides an added layer of security without detracting from your overall financial goals. When strategically managed, the liquidity, capital preservation, and growth opportunities of IUL policies create a robust foundation for both crisis management and wealth building.

However, it's critical to note that this strategy should be carefully tailored to your specific financial goals and risk tolerance, often with the guidance of a financial advisor or insurance professional. Appropriate funding levels and policy designs need to be strategically established to ensure that the policy can perform effectively as an emergency fund without diminishing its potential as a powerful wealth-building tool.

In conclusion, using an IUL policy as an emergency fund provides a sophisticated and efficient way to safeguard against life's uncertainties while simultaneously enhancing your financial landscape. As part of a comprehensive financial plan, it ensures that you stay both prepared for emergencies and on course toward long-term growth and security.

Buying a Home with Funds from an IUL Policy

Purchasing a home is one of the most significant financial goals many people face in their lifetime. It's a multi-faceted decision, requiring careful planning, budgeting, and a clear understanding of one's financial landscape. Indexed Universal Life (IUL) insurance can play an instrumental role in achieving this goal by providing a flexible, tax-advantaged source of funds for prospective homeowners. By leveraging the dynamics of cash value accumulation inherent in IUL policies, one can potentially secure the funds necessary to purchase a home without incurring the tax burdens typical of traditional withdrawal methods.

Leveraging the Cash Value

One of the foremost advantages of an IUL policy is its capacity to create cash value over time, linked to the performance of selected stock market indexes. This feature sets the stage for a robust savings mechanism, combining the growth potential of market indexes with the security of guaranteed minimum protection against loss. Through disciplined contributions and smart selection of index-linked crediting strategies, policyholders can amass a significant cash value that may be accessed via policy loans or withdrawals.

This cash value can be utilized as a down payment on a home, allowing policyholders to bypass the taxable consequences sometimes associated with withdrawing from other investment accounts such as 401(k)s or IRAs. Instead, funds borrowed from the cash value of an IUL are typically tax-free, as loans are not considered a taxable event by the IRS. This tax-advantaged liquidity is one of the crucial benefits that make IUL policies an attractive option for funding major purchases, such as a home.

Strategic Policy Loans

Borrowing against the cash value in an IUL policy is a popular strategy. When structured correctly, these loans can provide the needed liquidity for a down payment without depleting the cash value permanently or triggering taxable events. With historical loan interest rates often being relatively competitive, policyholders might find it financially more advantageous to borrow from their IUL than to liquidate other assets or incur additional debts.

A critical consideration when utilizing policy loans is the interest rate charged and how it compares to potential growth rates within the policy. If the interest rate on the loan is lower than the crediting rate on the remaining cash value, the policy owner can effectively fund their home purchase while continuing to see net-positive cash value growth.

Planning Considerations

To successfully leverage an IUL policy for home purchasing, meticulous planning is crucial. The first step is ensuring that the policy has been properly funded and managed over a sufficient period. Adequate cash value accumulation is necessary to support both the spending requirements and the continued viability of the post-loan policy. Regular contributions, mindful index selections, and optimization of policy features are essential to allowing cash value to grow sufficiently.

It's also important to assess the sustainability of loan repayment plans. While IUL loans offer flexibility, interest generation and compounding effects require careful monitoring to avoid excessive borrowing detrimental to the policy's longevity.

Case Study Example

Consider a hypothetical scenario: Jane, a professional in her mid-40s, began contributing to her IUL policy a decade ago. Through consistent premium payments and strategic index selections, her policy has developed a robust cash value. Jane identifies a desirable home and requires $50,000 for her down payment. Instead of withdrawing from her retirement accounts or taking a high-interest personal loan, she opts to take a loan against her IUL's cash value.

Her IUL policy's loan interest rate is set at 3.5%, while her policy's cash value has been averaging a crediting rate of about 5% over the past several years. By taking the loan, Jane effectively funds her new home purchase, continues to enjoy the protection and growth potential of her policy, and avoids triggering any immediate taxable income.

Using an IUL policy to fund a home purchase can be a highly effective strategy when crafted with foresight and diligence. The combination of tax advantages, flexible funding, and continued cash value growth positions IUL policies as a powerful tool to address major financial milestones like homeownership. However, success in this endeavor requires careful planning, ongoing portfolio management, and a firm grasp of the inherent financial dynamics. When approached correctly, an IUL policy not only aids in achieving the dream of homeownership but also serves as a cornerstone for continued financial security and wealth building.

Tax Implications and Long-term Impact of Using IUL to Fund Major Goals

As financial planners and consumers navigate the complex landscape of funding major financial goals, Indexed Universal Life (IUL) insurance presents a unique and multifaceted tool. This subpoint delves into the intricate tax implications and the long-term impact of using IUL to fund such major objectives. From retirement savings and college expenses to estate planning, understanding these components is crucial for capitalizing on the full potential of an IUL policy.

Tax Implications

One of the most compelling advantages of IUL is its tax-favored status. Primarily, the cash value accumulation within the policy grows tax deferred. This means that you won't face taxation on capital gains, interest, or dividends as long as the funds remain within the policy. Tax-deferred growth can be substantial over time, especially when compounded, providing a significant edge over traditional savings vehicles subject to annual taxation.

Upon withdrawal or taking policy loans, the tax implications can be navigated strategically. Policyholders can access their funds through loans or partial surrenders, typically up to the amount of premiums paid, without triggering any immediate income tax. This is because policy loans do not count as income. However, it's vital to manage these carefully to avoid policy lapses, which could lead to an immediate tax consequence on any outstanding loans that exceed the paid premiums.

IUL policies also offer a tax-free death benefit, a pivotal feature that ensures beneficiaries can receive the policy proceeds without income tax penalties. This can be especially critical in estate planning, where preserving wealth across generations is often a primary objective, and avoiding erosion from tax obligations is essential.

Long-term Impact

The long-term impact of using an IUL to fund major financial goals is profound. Let's consider retirement as a focal point. Given the tax-deferred nature of cash value growth, the potential for significant accumulation is enhanced, particularly when compared to other retirement savings options subjected to annual taxation. Importantly, the ability to withdraw funds tax-free through loans can supplement retirement income effectively, providing flexibility and potentially reducing the burdens on other retirement accounts that are subject to required minimum distributions.

For funding education, an IUL policy offers both growth potential and flexibility without the restrictions some education savings plans face, such as penalties for non-qualified withdrawals. The policy can be tailored to fit shifting educational needs and timelines, a valuable asset in the ever-evolving landscape of higher education costs.

Estate planning further underscores the efficacy of IUL policy. By providing a tax-free death benefit, policyholders can ensure that their financial legacy remains intact for heirs, effectively sidestepping the often-significant tax liabilities associated with other inheritance methods. Hence, IUL serves as a robust vehicle for transferring wealth across generations in a tax-efficient manner.

Moreover, the IUL framework permits policyholders to adjust in response to life's uncertainties. This adaptability extends through mechanisms such as varying premium payments and adjusting death benefits, ensuring that as financial goals change, the policy can be realigned accordingly. This inherent flexibility allows IUL users to capitalize on potential market upswings while enjoying a guaranteed floor, which shields against total market-based losses—a blend of growth opportunity and security not easily found elsewhere.

Finally, considering the role of inflation in long-term planning, the IUL's strategy of linking to a market index, such as the S&P 500, can help the cash value keep pace with inflationary pressures, a crucial consideration in both retirement planning and college funding. It's worth noting that while the policy absorbs market gains up to a specified cap, it provides downside protection in bear markets, ensuring the original capital isn't depleted by market volatility.

In synthesis, IUL stands out as a nuanced and dynamic strategy for funding major financial goals with significant tax advantages and long-term viability. By providing a facility for tax-deferred growth, flexible tax-free withdrawals, and a potent vehicle for estate planning all wrapped within the protective blanket of life insurance benefits, IUL offers a compelling proposition. Ultimately, leveraging these features judiciously and in concert with personal financial goals can offer security, growth, and legacy-building potential that few other products can match, making it a keystone in a well-rounded financial plan.

Chapter 7_Wealth Building Strategies with IUL

To unlock the full potential of an Indexed Universal Life (IUL) policy in wealth-building, it is imperative to start with a detailed evaluation of your financial goals and current needs. This initial assessment forms the bedrock upon which all subsequent strategies are constructed. Only through a comprehensive understanding of your financial landscape can you effectively leverage the unique benefits of IUL.

Assessing Income Stability

Income stability is a critical factor in determining the right IUL strategy for you. It affects both your ability to consistently contribute to the policy and your capacity to withstand potential financial downturns. Start with a thorough review of your income sources: Are you predominantly salaried, self-employed, or do you rely on other income streams such as rental properties? Consider the reliability and potential fluctuations of these income sources. For instance, a salaried employee with a stable job and predictable income may opt for a more aggressive contribution strategy due to lower income risk. Conversely, someone with variable income might prioritize flexibility in premiums to accommodate income fluctuations.

Understanding Your Tax Situation

IULs are particularly attractive for their tax-advantaged growth potential. Conduct a detailed analysis of your current tax bracket and anticipate changes in your tax situation. This involves understanding how your income, deductions, and credits affect your tax liabilities. Suppose you are currently in a high tax bracket but anticipate a lower one at retirement; in this scenario, maximizing contributions while deferring taxes through an IUL could be beneficial. However, if you expect to remain in a high bracket, exploiting tax-free loans and withdrawals during retirement might hold more appeal.

Projecting Future Financial Needs

Future financial needs are as diverse as they are crucial. They range from funding children's education to securing a comfortable retirement. Begin by listing your anticipated major expenses and their timelines. How do you plan to fund these needs? IULs can serve as a versatile tool in your portfolio, providing liquidity through loans without triggering taxes. Map out scenarios—craft a plan for retiring at 65 with enough income to support your lifestyle for 30 years, or for saving an adequate sum for a child's college education. Realistically estimate costs and consider the role an IUL might play in achieving these objectives, offering both protection and growth.

Evaluating Risk Tolerance

An understanding of your risk tolerance is fundamental when selecting an appropriate IUL policy. IULs tie cash value accumulation to market indexes, thus introducing varying degrees of risk and opportunity. Assess how comfortable you are with market-linked growth and the potential for variability in returns. Are you more conservative, preferring the security of downside protection, or are you willing to engage with more aggressive indexing options for the chance at greater returns? Recognize that your policy choice should align with your broader risk profile—balancing growth with security.

Setting Realistic Financial Goals

After evaluating these factors, set clear, achievable financial goals. Use SMART criteria: Specific, Measurable, Achievable, Relevant, and Time-bound. Instead of vague ambitions like "build wealth," aim for a goal such as "Accumulate $500,000 through an IUL by age 60 to supplement retirement income." Break these goals into stages and periodically revisit them to track progress and adjust to any life changes.

Real-World Examples

Consider Alisha, a single professional in her 30s with stable income and high tax obligations. Her goal might involve using an IUL as an additional retirement income pillar, benefiting from tax-free withdrawals post-retirement. On the other hand, Tom and Susan, with two young children and an appetite for risk, might utilize an IUL to generate tax-advantaged growth while securing their children's education fund.

Meanwhile, Pedro, a self-employed consultant with fluctuating earnings, might focus on the policy's premium flexibility and potential for tax-deferred growth without locking into overly ambitious contribution commitments. For each of these individuals, their differing backgrounds dictate distinct IUL strategies reflecting their financial realities and aspirations.

Ultimately, setting the stage with a thorough assessment of your financial goals and current situation lays the groundwork for a robust IUL strategy tailored to your unique needs. By understanding your income, taxes, future needs, and risk disposition, you are better positioned to maximize the benefits of IUL and work towards financial security and prosperity.</

Selecting the Right IUL Policy: Navigating Features, Costs, and Providers

Choosing the right Indexed Universal Life (IUL) policy is an essential step in your journey towards building tax-advantaged wealth. While IULs present a unique opportunity to grow your wealth through their combination of life insurance and market-linked growth potential, the differences across various policies can significantly impact your financial outcomes. This section aims to guide you through the maze of policy features, cost structures, and provider options, ensuring you make an informed and effective decision.

Understanding Key Policy Features

First and foremost, it is critical to identify the IUL policy features that resonate with your financial goals. IUL policies are inherently flexible, allowing you to customize them to suit your needs. Key features to consider include:

1. **Indexing Options:** Evaluate the market indices that the policy is tied to. Policies often offer a selection of indices like the S&P 500, giving you the ability to choose one that matches your risk tolerance and expected market outlook.

2. **Participation Rates and Caps:** These are limits on how much of the index gains your policy can participate in. Policies with higher participation rates and caps will generally offer more growth potential

but must be assessed within the context of potential risks.

3. **Guaranteed Floor Rates:** IULs typically provide a guaranteed minimum rate of return, which is crucial for protection during market downturns. Understanding these floor rates helps ensure that the policy aligns with your need for security.

4. **Loan Features and Withdrawal Options:** Many policies allow you to borrow against the cash value. Understand the terms, interest rates, and repercussions of withdrawing or borrowing, as these can affect your policy's long-term value.

Navigating the Cost Structure

The cost structure of an IUL can be complex, encompassing various fees and charges that can erode your cash value if not carefully managed. It is essential to comprehend these costs upfront:

1. **Premium Charges:** Initial premium payments can have loading fees deducted, which cover the insurer's expenses. Understanding these can help in comparing the net amount that contributes to your cash value.

2. **Cost of Insurance (COI):** This ongoing fee increases with age and can significantly impact the policy's cash value. Reviewing the COI trajectory is critical in assessing the policy's affordability in the long run.

3. **Administrative and Surrender Charges:** These are fees related to policy maintenance and early policy termination. Assessing these charges ensures that the policy can withstand potential lifestyle or financial changes without prohibitive costs.

4. **Rider Fees:** Additional benefits, like long-term care or critical illness riders, can provide extra protection but come with associated costs. It's essential to weigh these benefits against their fees to determine their value.

Comparing IUL Offerings

With a clear understanding of the features and costs, the next step is to compare IUL offerings. Here's a practical approach:

1. **Use Comparison Tools:** Leverage online calculators and comparison tools to input your financial goals and receive tailored policy analyses. These tools are instrumental in providing a side-by-side comparison of different offerings.

2. **Consult Financial Advisors:** Engage with a financial advisor who specializes in IULs. Their expertise can offer insights into complex policy elements and provide advice personalized to your financial landscape.

3. **Review Case Studies:** Examine real-world examples and testimonials of successful IUL policyholders. Learning from others' experiences can highlight potential pitfalls and successful strategies.

Selecting a Reputable Provider

Choosing the right insurance provider is as critical as selecting the policy itself. Consider the following tips:

1. **Check Financial Stability:** Research the insurer's financial health through ratings from agencies like A.M. Best or Standard & Poor's. A strong financial standing ensures the company's ability to meet its long-term obligations.

2. **Assess Customer Service:** A provider's reputation for customer service can impact on your overall policy experience. Look for insurers with high customer satisfaction scores and positive testimonials.

3. **Understand Their Track Record:** Analyze the provider's history with IUL products. Experienced providers with a proven record of offering reliable policies tend to be more trustworthy.

Real Case Studies

To illustrate, consider the example of a family who successfully secured their financial future through a well-chosen IUL policy. By identifying a policy with robust growth features and cost-effective insurance charges, they capitalized on a reputable provider's track record. Their strategic indexing option and careful monitoring of costs allowed them to maximize policy growth while maintaining peace of mind through comprehensive coverage.

In conclusion, the process of selecting the right IUL policy requires careful consideration of your financial goals, cost evaluation, effective comparisons, and provider research. With this comprehensive approach, you can make an informed decision that aligns with your wealth-building aspirations while providing essential financial security.

Funding Strategies for Your IUL Policy

To effectively harness the wealth-building potential of an Indexed Universal Life (IUL) policy, understanding and meticulously planning how you fund your policy is a foundational step.

An IUL policy offers unparalleled flexibility in how premiums are structured, allowing you to tailor a financial plan that aligns with both short- and long-term goals. By navigating this dynamic landscape judiciously, you can enhance the cash value accumulation and ultimately leverage the policy's benefits to fortify your wealth strategy.

Understanding Premium Flexibility

One of the most appealing aspects of IUL is the premium flexibility it offers. Unlike traditional life insurance policies, IULs allow policyholders to adjust premium payments, which can be an incredibly strategic tool when managed wisely. This flexibility means you have the option to pay more in good financial years, thereby accelerating the growth of your policy's cash value. In leaner times, you can opt to reduce payments to the minimum necessary to keep the policy active.

For example, Jay, a 45-year-old entrepreneur, found himself with significant surplus cash in several profitable years. Instead of simply pocketing the surplus, Jay significantly increased his premiums during those years. As a result, his cash value grew exponentially, giving him a robust financial buffer during economic downturns when he opted to minimize his premium outlay.

Lump Sum vs. Periodic Payments

When funding your IUL, deciding between a lump sum payment and periodic payments is a pivotal choice. Both approaches have distinct advantages and can significantly impact the growth trajectory of your policy's cash value.

Lump Sum Payment: Opting for a lump sum payment can be advantageous if you come into a substantial amount of money, such as an inheritance or a major bonus. By funding the policy upfront, you'll potentially jumpstart the accumulation of cash value, benefiting from market index-linked returns sooner. This proactive funding method can maximize compounding benefits while also offering peace of mind knowing your policy is comfortably funded.

Periodic Payments: Most policyholders opt for regular, periodic payments that fit seamlessly into their financial routines. This method offers stability of ongoing growth and can often align well with cash flow planning. Christine, a 38-year-old financial analyst, adopted this strategy by setting up monthly payments that were convenient for her budgeting style. This regular approach allowed her to evenly distribute her financial commitments while steadily building her policy's value.

Using Riders to Enhance Policy Value

Riders are powerful add-ons that can significantly enhance the coverage and benefits of an IUL policy. While riders can come at an additional cost, they provide tailored enhancements that can align the policy more closely with individual needs.

For instance, the "over loan protection rider" can guard against a policy lapse if you've extensively borrowed against your policy. Another popular option is the "accelerated benefits rider," which allows you to access a portion of the death benefit in the event of a chronic or terminal illness. These riders can be integral in providing additional security and flexibility while funding the IUL, giving you the latitude to adapt the policy as life circumstances change.

Strategic Funding Approaches: Real-World Examples

Consider the case of Linda and Mark, a couple in their early 50s who wanted to maximize their retirement savings using an IUL policy. They decided on a phased approach: for the first ten years, they allocated part of their annual bonuses to pay higher premiums, benefiting from considerable tax-deferred growth. Their strategic funding choice enabled them to use policy loans as a tax-free source of income during retirement, all while maintaining the death benefit for their heirs.

On the other hand, Michael, a solo practitioner lawyer, chose to fund his IUL policy through quarterly payments that coincided with his natural cash flow cycles. By aligning his funding strategy with his income peaks, he effectively managed his cash flow while ensuring consistent, substantial growth of his policy's cash value.

When navigating an IUL policy, the key to substantial wealth building lies in choosing and executing the right funding strategy. Whether you opt for lump sum contributions, periodic payments, or strategically deploy riders, each decision should align with your personal financial landscape and long-term goals. By meticulously planning your premium payments and harnessing the full flexibility and future-forward benefits of an IUL policy, you'll be well-positioned not just to accumulate wealth but to secure a financially vibrant future.

Integrating an Indexed Universal Life (IUL) into Your Financial Plan

Integrating an Indexed Universal Life (IUL) insurance policy into a comprehensive financial plan requires a strategic approach that considers your entire financial landscape. The versatile nature of IUL allows it to play multiple roles, from providing a death benefit to offering a reservoir of tax-advantaged cash value growth. However, its true potential is unleashed when it's aligned with your broader financial strategy, covering retirement planning, estate planning, and even emergency funds.

Harmonizing IUL with Retirement Planning

An IUL policy can serve as a cornerstone of your retirement planning. One of the key benefits of an IUL is its ability to accumulate cash value over time, which can be tapped into during your retirement years. The cash value grows tax-deferred, and if structured properly, policy loans or withdrawals can be accessed tax-free. This setup can act as a supplementary income stream during retirement, complementing traditional vehicles like 401(k)s or IRAs.

Incorporating an IUL into your retirement plan involves assessing your long-term income goals and understanding how the IUL's cash value can fill potential gaps. It is important to evaluate your risk tolerance and financial goals. While stocks and other securities may offer high returns, they also come with risks. An IUL provides a safety net with its downside protection features. If the market dips, the IUL will safeguard your principal, ensuring your retirement funds are protected.

IUL in Estate Planning

Beyond retirement, an IUL policy is a strategic tool in estate planning. One of its primary benefits is the ability to provide a tax-free death benefit. This can be particularly advantageous for individuals looking to leave a financial legacy for their heirs. When integrating IUL into your estate plan, the policy's death benefit can be used to cover estate taxes, ensuring that your assets are passed on to your beneficiaries intact.

Furthermore, the cash value in an IUL policy offers liquidity that can be crucial in estate planning. It can provide your estate with immediate cash upon your passing, avoiding the potential need to liquidate other estate assets in a rush or unfavorable terms to cover costs. This liquidity ensures that your estate is settled efficiently and that your beneficiaries receive the maximum intended benefit.

Building a Safety Net with IUL

An IUL policy can also act as a financial cushion in times of emergency. By leveraging the cash value component, policyholders have access to funds that can be crucial in unexpected situations such as medical emergencies or sudden loss of income. While the death benefit is the destination for the worst-case scenario, the living benefits of the cash value help in bridging gaps throughout life's unforeseen events.

However, it is imperative to balance this with your broader emergency fund strategy. Traditional savings accounts or money market funds should still form the first line of defense due to their liquidity and lack of withdrawal penalties. An IUL, although liquid, should be reserved for larger or longer-term financial emergencies where its access terms are more favorable than hastily liquidating investment assets.

Balancing IUL with Other Financial Instruments

The key to effective financial planning is balance. While an IUL is multifaceted, it should complement, not compete with, other financial instruments in your portfolio. Regular reviews and assessments of your financial plan are crucial. This includes evaluating returns, fees, and risks associated with all investment vehicles, including your IUL.

Diversification is fundamental. Your portfolio should not only balance between different investment vehicles but also between risk and return. An IUL can be a stable component amidst more volatile investments, offering growth potential without directly exposing you to market risks.

Visualizing and Achieving Success with IUL

Success in integrating an IUL policy within your financial plan can be vividly illustrated through diagrams and real-life success stories. Diagrams can help visualize cash flows, policy loans, and the interplay of IUL with other financial instruments within your plan. Success stories provide tangible examples of strategies that have worked, allowing you to model your approach after proven methodologies.

For instance, consider a couple who utilized their IUL to balance investment risk, ensuring retirement income stability while leaving a substantial legacy. Their story might highlight how they structured their IUL to align with their other investments, ensuring a dynamic yet stable approach to wealth accumulation and legacy planning.

Integrating an IUL within a comprehensive financial plan requires foresight and continual evaluation. By positioning your IUL strategically across retirement, estate, and contingency planning, and ensuring it aligns with your financial goals and risk tolerance, you create a resilient, adaptive financial plan capable of weathering life's uncertainties while maximizing your wealth-building potential.

Monitoring and Adapting Your IUL Investment

When embarking on your wealth-building journey with an Indexed Universal Life (IUL) insurance policy, understanding the importance of ongoing monitoring and adaptability is crucial—not merely as a means of maintenance but as a proactive approach to maximizing your policy's potential. An IUL, like any premier financial instrument, is not a "set it and forget it" affair. Instead, it requires continuous attention, refinement, and adaptability to align with both market shifts and personal milestones. In this discussion, we will explore practical strategies to monitor your IUL performance, interpret essential reports, and make informed adjustments that align with your evolving financial landscape.

Reviewing Your IUL Performance

The foundation of any successful IUL strategy lies in regularly reviewing your policy's performance. This involves assessing the cash value accumulation, the cost of insurance, and any associated fees. The cash value of your IUL is linked to specific indexes—you may choose popular ones like the S&P 500, NASDAQ, or a collection of international indexes. It's essential to understand how these indexes are performing and how they impact your policy. Insurance companies typically provide annual statements detailing your policy's cash value, death benefit, and available borrowing amount. Scrutinize these reports to observe trends, both in growth and expenses.

Interpreting Insurance Provider Reports

A critical aspect of monitoring your IUL policy is effectively interpreting the reports provided by your insurance provider. These reports can be intricate, often filled with industry jargon and numbers that may seem overwhelming at first glance. Understanding key metrics such as the policy's interest crediting rate, the performance of underlying indexes, and the substance of any policy loans taken is vital. Regularly reviewing these details not only helps in assessing the current performance but also informs future projections. Remember, clarity on these reports is not a luxury but a necessity—don't hesitate to seek clarification from your insurance provider or financial advisor when needed.

Making Necessary Adjustments

Adapting your IUL policy in response to changes is as much an art as it is a science. Adjustments may be required due to personal milestones—such as marriage, the birth of a child, or retirement—or shifts in financial goals. For instance, as you approach retirement, you may wish to shift priorities from aggressive growth to preservation of capital. Adjustments could include altering premium allocations, reconsidering index selections, or modifying the death benefit to suit new financial responsibilities. Equally, market conditions, economic forecasts, and changes in tax legislation should prompt you to review and potentially adjust your strategy.

Staying Informed About Market and Regulatory Changes

To maximize the effectiveness of your IUL policy, staying informed about market trends and regulatory changes is indispensable. Market volatility and economic policies can influence index performance significantly, which in turn impacts the growth of your policy's cash value. Moreover, modifications in tax laws can alter the advantages associated with policy loans and tax-free distributions. Maintain a habit of staying updated through financial news outlets, webinars from financial advisors, and insights from your insurance company. By staying informed, you empower yourself to make proactive decisions rather than reactive corrections.

Learning from Real-World Adaptations

The power of adaptability is best illustrated through real-world examples. Consider a policyholder who, during the tech boom, reallocated his index exposure towards a technology-heavy index, thereby capturing significant gains that contributed to a robust cash value accumulation. Conversely, another policyholder, foreseeing potential economic downturns, opted to minimize exposure to volatile indexes, thereby safeguarding their principal. Both instances exemplify how proactive strategies lead to substantial benefits and security.

Incorporating relentless vigilance and adaptability into your IUL investment strategy is not a mere suggestion; it is a necessity for achieving long-term financial success. By diligently monitoring your policy, interpreting provider reports accurately, adjusting your strategy to align with personal and market changes, and staying informed about the broader financial landscape, you fortify your investment's resilience against unforeseen challenges. Embrace the proactive stewardship of your IUL, and you will harness its full potential to achieve your financial aspirations.

Exit Strategies and Legacy Planning with IUL

Incorporating Indexed Universal Life (IUL) insurance into your financial strategy is a dynamic approach to wealth-building, providing both growth potential and protection. However, as with any financial instrument, having a well-considered exit strategy is crucial to ensure that your wealth-building journey aligns with your long-term objectives. Exit strategies are not only about liquidating assets; they also entail planning for efficient wealth transfer, potentially enhancing one's legacy. Here's how you can navigate the complexities of exit strategies and legacy planning with IUL.

Crafting an Exit Strategy for IUL Policies

An exit strategy with an IUL policy primarily involves understanding the tax implications and financial impact of withdrawals, policy loans, and policy surrender. Each choice can significantly affect your financial landscape, so let's explore these in detail.

1. **Policy Loans and Withdrawals:** IUL policies allow for policy loans and withdrawals against the cash value. These are often touted as tax-free because they are considered a loan, not income. However, it is essential to maintain an appropriate balance. Excessive borrowing can erode the death benefit and even result in policy lapse if the loan accruement surpasses the cash value. Including a repayment plan in your financial strategy might prove beneficial to sustain the policy's benefits and your wealth-building trajectory.

2. **Policy Surrender:** If you've decided not to maintain the policy, you may choose to surrender it. While this action provides immediate cash, it comes with potential tax liabilities on any gains. Moreover, surrendering cancels the death benefit, eliminating a potential tool for wealth transfer and legacy planning. Thus, understanding the tax implications and

aligning this step with your broader financial goals is of paramount importance.

Leveraging IUL for Legacy Planning

Legacy planning with IUL policies is an astute strategy for transferring wealth efficiently and can achieve this through tax-advantaged mechanisms. Here's how to utilize your IUL policy for securing a legacy:

1. **Tax-Efficient Wealth Transfer:** One of the standout features of IUL policies is the tax-free death benefit. When a policyholder passes away, beneficiaries receive the death benefit without the burden of income tax, making this an excellent way to secure the financial future of your loved ones. Structuring the policy correctly can maximize the amount passed on to heirs, sidestepping potential tax burdens and probate delays.

2. **Estate Equalization:** In families where asset distribution could potentially create discord—like in businesses or real estate holdings—IUL can serve as an equalization tool. The death benefit can be distributed to heirs who will not inherit certain tangible assets, balancing the estate distribution and maintaining family harmony.

3. **Charitable Giving:** For those interested in philanthropy, IUL can be a vehicle for tax-efficient charitable contributions. Through the IUL policy, you can ensure that part of your wealth contributes to a cause dear to you without diminishing the estate value passed on to your heirs.

Real-Life Examples of IUL Legacy Planning

Consider the example of the Thompson family, who utilized IUL as part of their wealth transfer strategy. Mr. and Mrs. Thompson owned a successful business. To keep the family business within the family without causing inequity among their children, they opted to use IUL policies. They directed the bulk of the business inheritance to their two children involved in the company. Simultaneously, they provided an equivalent value through IUL death benefits to their other children who weren't involved in the business. This method not only precluded potential family disputes but optimized the effective use of their estate for future generations.

Similarly, the Lewis family, who had substantial real estate holdings, faced challenges distributing their estate tax-efficiently. By including IUL in their estate planning, they were able to leverage its tax-free death benefits to cover estate taxes, allowing heirs to inherit real estate holdings without the need to liquidate assets to pay taxes.

Preparing for the future with IUL means more than just growing your wealth; it involves strategically planning your approach to exit and legacy. With a deep understanding of your options—loans, withdrawals, surrender, and legacy benefits—you can craft an exit strategy that aligns with your aspirations, whether they're ensuring a comfortable retirement or securing your family's financial future. By leveraging the unique features of IUL policies, you can not only meet today's financial goals but also leave a lasting legacy of fiscal wisdom and security.

Chapter 8_Maximizing Wealth with IUL

Understanding the Foundations of IUL for Wealth Building

Building wealth with Indexed Universal Life (IUL) insurance requires a thorough understanding of the foundational mechanics that govern these unique financial tools. At its core, an IUL policy not only provides a death benefit but also serves as a flexible wealth-building instrument with opportunities for tax-advantaged growth. Let's delve into the essential components that make IULs a formidable ally in your wealth accumulation strategies.

Premium Allocation and Its Strategic Implications

When you purchase an IUL policy, you commit to paying premiums which are then allocated between the insurance cost and the cash value component. The unique aspect of IUL policies is their flexibility, allowing you to adjust premium payments over time. This flexibility can be a powerful wealth-building tool. By strategically increasing your premium contributions, especially during high-income years, you can significantly boost the policy's cash value. Conversely, during leaner times, the ability to reduce or even skip premium payments without sacrificing coverage adds a layer of financial resilience.

The Role of the Cash Value Component

A pivotal feature of IUL policies is the cash value account, which grows over time and can be accessed for various financial needs. The growth potential of this account is what underpins the wealth-building aspect of IULs. Unlike other insurance products, the cash value in an IUL is linked to a market index, offering potentially higher returns without directly investing in the stock market. This linkage provides policyholders with upside growth potential while safeguarding the principal during market downturns. As the cash value builds, it becomes a resource you can tap for tax-free policy loans or withdrawals, thus transforming the policy into a financial workhorse capable of funding retirement, education, or other significant expenses.

Indexing Method for Crediting Interest

One of the distinctive features of IUL policies is how they credit interest to your cash value. The interest credited is based on the performance of a chosen stock market index, such as the S&P 500. However, policyholders aren't investing directly in the stock market, which insulates them from market losses. Instead, these policies utilize a method known as indexing, where the positive performance of the index up to a cap rate is credited to the cash value. This mechanism allows you to enjoy gains up to a certain percentage, while still protecting your cash from negative index returns, making it a vital component for steady, long-term wealth growth.

Choosing the Right Index Options

Selecting the appropriate index options for your IUL policy is crucial for maximizing wealth accumulation. Most IUL policies offer multiple index choices, each with different cap rates, participation rates, and fees. It's essential to assess these options based on historical performance, current economic conditions, and your risk tolerance. Diversifying your policy by tying different portions of your cash value to various indexes can also spread risk and potentially enhance returns. Working with a knowledgeable financial advisor can help you navigate these choices, ensuring your selections align with your financial goals and risk appetite.

Understanding the Cost of Insurance Within the IUL Framework

While IULs offer substantial advantages for wealth accumulation, it's imperative to understand the cost of insurance (COI) involved. COI is the charge deducted from your premiums that cover the death benefit. These charges typically increase with age, reducing the net return on your cash value. Therefore, it's beneficial to fund your policy adequately early on to leverage compound growth of your cash value, which can offset rising insurance costs as you age. Transparent awareness of these costs and their impact on your cash value is critical for effective policy management.

In conclusion, understanding the foundations of IUL insurance involves a deep dive into its premium allocation, cash value mechanics, and the indexing methods for crediting interest. Each of these elements plays a vital role in harnessing the full potential of an IUL policy as a cornerstone of your wealth-building strategy. By comprehensively understanding these components, choosing the appropriate index options, and managing insurance costs diligently, you set the stage for a robust and resilient financial future. As you incorporate IUL into your broader financial plan, you can unlock its multifaceted benefits to achieve and sustain your long-term financial goals, all while preserving the promise of a legacy for future generations.

Starting an IUL Policy: Strategic Considerations

Embarking on an Indexed Universal Life (IUL) policy journey is akin to setting the foundation for a multi-story financial structure. Done thoughtfully, it can provide not only safety and protection but also a pathway to significant wealth growth. Your task is to ensure that you begin this journey with clarity and strategic foresight, understanding the nuances that can make or break the potential of your IUL policy in the long run.

Determining Coverage Amount

The first step in initiating an IUL policy is to determine the appropriate coverage amount. This decision hinges on your financial goals and personal needs—both immediate and future. Ask yourself: what do you aim to protect or accomplish with this IUL policy? Whether it's providing for family income replacement, covering debts, or funding future goals like education and retirement, your coverage amount should align with your overarching financial objectives.

Consider conducting a thorough needs analysis, often with the help of a financial advisor, to quantify the desired coverage. This analysis should encompass all pertinent factors, such as your current financial status, anticipated changes in lifestyle, future liabilities, and any existing insurance coverage.

Deciding on Premium Payments

Next, you'll need to consider how to structure your premium payments. IUL policies offer flexibility, allowing you to adjust premiums over time, which can be particularly beneficial as your financial situation evolves.

When strategizing premium payments, you have the choice between lump-sum funding—where you inject a significant amount of money upfront—and periodic payments, which involve regularly scheduled contributions. Each method has its merits. Lump-sum funding allows for immediate cash value accumulation, which can be advantageous in leveraging the policy's growth potential. Conversely, periodic payments allow for more manageable, consistent contributions that can align with your cash flow and budgeting preferences.

One key consideration is ensuring your premium payments are continually maximized within the limits set forth by IRS guidelines to avoid your policy being classified as a Modified Endowment Contract (MEC), which could trigger unfavorable tax implications.

Understanding Rider Options

Riders can be powerful tools in customizing your IUL policy, enhancing its utility, and providing additional coverage. Whether it's accelerated death benefit riders, long-term care riders, or waiver of premium riders, each option should be considered in the context of your personal and financial circumstances.

Accelerated death benefit riders can be invaluable in cases of terminal illness, allowing you to access a portion of the death benefit while you're still alive. Long-term care riders may provide a solution for potential healthcare needs, thereby preventing the need to draw from other savings. Evaluate which riders complement your financial plan and offer the protections you envision needing in the future.

Optimizing Policies for Financial Growth

Optimization should be at the core of any IUL policy strategy. Here, balancing cash value growth against insurance costs is key. Recognize that the most effective IUL policies are those where substantial funds are allocated towards the cash value component. The idea is to capture the benefits of index-linked growth while preserving the tax-deferred structure of the policy.

Work closely with your financial advisor to ensure the policy is structured to maximize growth potential while mitigating any potential risks. This requires regular reviews, wherein you assess performance against projections and adjust elements like the death benefit and premium payments as needed.

Funding Methods and Timing Considerations

Deciding on the best funding method and timing your entry into the IUL market are strategic elements that require due diligence. If considering a lump-sum payment, assess the current market environment to ensure that such an investment aligns with broader economic conditions. As markets ebb and flow, it's wise to enter when market conditions are favorable for growth.

Alternatively, if opting for periodic payments, consistency is crucial. Establishing and adhering to a well-structured payment schedule ensures continual cash value growth within your policy. Additionally, staying attuned to market trends and adjusting payment amounts during favorable periods can further enhance growth.

Timing is not merely about recognizing external market conditions but also understanding internal readiness. When entering the market, consider your holistic financial situation, future income stability, and any major lifestyle changes on the horizon. By aligning your entry with both market conditions and personal readiness, you position your IUL policy for optimal performance from the outset.

In conclusion, the initiation of an IUL policy is a deliberate process requiring careful diligence and strategic planning. By thoughtfully considering coverage amounts, payment structures, riders, and funding methods, you are laying a robust foundation for leveraging the powerful benefits of IUL policies—enabling them to serve as a cornerstone of your long-term wealth-building strategy.

Real-world Examples of Successful IUL Wealth-Building Strategies

When navigating the intricate world of Indexed Universal Life (IUL) insurance, real-world examples provide a tangible reflection of the potential these policies hold for building wealth. These case studies illustrate how the strategic deployment of IUL policies can align with individual financial goals, leveraging their unique features to yield significant benefits. Here, we explore three diverse examples of successful IUL strategies, providing insights into the versatility and practical application of IUL in wealth building.

Case Study 1: Retiree Seeking Stable Income

Meet Sarah, a 55-year-old corporate executive inching toward retirement with a desire for stable, tax-efficient income during her golden years. With the advice of her financial advisor, Sarah incorporated an IUL policy into her financial strategy. Her primary goals were preserving capital and ensuring a tax-free income stream post-retirement.

Features Utilized:

- **Indexing Flexibility:** Sarah's IUL policy was linked to the S&P 500, allowing her to capitalize on market upswings while safeguarding her principal during downturns.

- **Tax-free Loans and Withdrawals:** To support her retirement, Sarah planned for tax-free policy loans, thus minimizing her taxable income.

- **Lifetime Income Benefit Riders:** To ensure a steady income, Sarah opted for a lifetime income benefit rider, adding a level of assurance to her retirement plan.

Outcomes:

- Upon retirement, Sarah's IUL policy began to provide a consistent tax-free income stream through policy loans. The indexing strategy protected the policy's cash value during market downturns, and the lifetime income rider ensured that Sarah wouldn't outlive her resources.

Consequently, she enjoyed a financially secure and worry-free retirement, with her initial capital still intact, enabling the legacy she intended for her heirs.

Case Study 2: Entrepreneur's Legacy Plan

John and Lisa, entrepreneurial parents in their mid-forties, wanted to establish a solid financial foundation that would ensure their children's future and provide business continuity. Their objectives included funding their children's education, mitigating estate taxes, and protecting their business assets.

Features Utilized:

- **Death Benefits:** The couple utilized the IUL's death benefit to its full potential, planning it as a wealth transfer tool to fund their children's education and mitigate potential estate taxes.

- **Cash Value Accumulation:** They leveraged the policy's cash value growth to fund opportunities for business expansion.

Outcomes:

- When John unfortunately passed away unexpectedly, the IUL policy's death benefit came into immediate effect, allowing for the smooth transfer of assets without the burden of estate taxes. The children's education was fully funded, and Lisa, remaining in the business, capitalized on the policy's accumulated cash value to expand the business as per their long-term plans. Their foresight ensured not only the fulfillment of family and business aspirations but also a lasting legacy.

Case Study 3: Young Professional's Wealth-Building Catalyst

Emma, a 30-year-old professional, was focused on long-term wealth accumulation and desired a flexible savings vehicle that offered both growth potential and protection. While traditional retirement savings routes were considered, Emma chose to include an IUL policy as a supplementary strategy to her financial plan.

Features Utilized:

- **Premium Flexibility:** The flexible premium structure allowed Emma to increase contributions in years where she had excess income, thereby maximizing her policy's cash value growth.

- **Participating Loans:** Emma planned to leverage participating loans in the future to initiate investments in real estate.

Outcomes:

- Emma's proactive contributions amplified her policy's cash value. After a decade, she used participating loans to purchase rental properties, simultaneously securing passive income and increasing her net worth. The flexibility to adjust her strategy in response to life changes - a feature intrinsic to IULs - proved essential. Emma's IUL policy acted not only as a security blanket but as a launching pad for broader wealth creation opportunities.

These real-world scenarios highlight the diverse applications and successes of IUL policies, underscoring their potential as a versatile financial tool. By tailoring IUL features to individual needs, clients like Sarah, John and Lisa, and Emma reaped significant benefits. Whether seeking retirement income, securing a family legacy, or building long-term wealth, the strategic use of IUL policies provides a foundation upon which financial dreams can flourish. As demonstrated, the careful orchestration of IUL features can indeed transform aspirations into reality, showcasing that with the right strategy, possibilities are expansive, and impact is profound.

Monitoring and Adjusting Your IUL Policy

When it comes to maximizing the potential of an Indexed Universal Life (IUL) policy, vigilance and adaptability are key. Just as in any other financial endeavor, a set-and-forget approach seldom yields optimal results. Instead, consider your IUL policy as a dynamic tool that requires regular tuning and adjustments to align with your evolving financial landscape and life goals. Here are some expert tips for regular monitoring and adjusting of your IUL policy to ensure it continually works to your advantage.

Emphasize the Importance of Annual Reviews

The cornerstone of effectively managing your IUL policy is routine evaluation. Annual reviews with your insurance professional or financial advisor should be a non-negotiable component of your financial planning calendar. These reviews allow you to assess the policy's performance in relation to the assumptions and projections made at the time of purchase. Reviewing your policy annually helps you identify discrepancies between actual and projected cash values, evaluate interest crediting rates, and examine how recent market performances have influenced your policy.

Moreover, annual check-ins offer an opportunity to reassess the policy's alignment with your financial goals. Life is fluid—your objectives, financial circumstances, and priorities can shift dramatically. As these changes, it's essential to ensure that your IUL policy remains a relevant piece of your financial puzzle.

Methods for Rebalancing Allocations

One of the distinctive features of an IUL policy is the flexibility to allocate your premium across different index accounts. Just as you would diversify a stock portfolio, it's important to consider periodic rebalancing of your IUL allocations. During your annual review, take an analytical look at the current index strategies you are invested in. Assess recent performance, market trends, and—perhaps most crucially—your risk tolerance, which might evolve with your age and changing financial scenario.

Diversify allocations among different index options or consider adjusting your participation rate and cap rates to align with the prevailing market conditions. For instance, in a bullish market, allocating more towards an index with broader participation may be beneficial, whereas in a volatile environment, you might favor options that include protective strategies like a floor or minimum guarantee.

Reactive Strategies to Life Events

Life doesn't happen in a vacuum, nor should your IUL policy remain static amidst personal and financial changes. Significant life events— such as marriage, the birth of a child, career shifts, or nearing retirement—warrant a revisit to your IUL policy. These transitions might call for an adjustment in your death benefit or a re-evaluation of your premium contributions to reflect newfound responsibilities or goals.

For new parents, increasing policy contributions could help fund future college savings through a tax-advantaged growth vehicle. Conversely, someone entering retirement might focus on optimizing their IUL to supplement income while minimizing taxes. Regularly updating your policy to reflect life changes ensures it remains an effective component of your comprehensive financial strategy.

Adapting to Economic Changes

Economic conditions, much like life, are continuously shifting. Interest rates, inflation, and market volatility can all impact policy performance. Regularly assess the economic environment as part of your IUL strategy. For instance, in a low-interest-rate settings, you might need to compensate for lower credit rates by re-evaluating the index selections or premium allocations.

Stay abreast of economic trends, tax law changes, and adjustments in insurance regulations that could affect your policy. Engage with financial news or consult your advisor to derive strategies that protect the policy's value while seizing opportunities that arise from these economic fluctuations.

Team Up with Your Advisor

Your financial advisor is a critical ally in navigating the complexities of an IUL policy. Their expertise not only ensures that you're making informed decisions during reviews and adjustments, but also that you're leveraging your policy effectively throughout its lifespan. Forge a proactive relationship with your advisor where dialogue is frequent, whether prompted by annual reviews or necessitated by a significant change in personal circumstances or the economic landscape.

In conclusion, the journey to building wealth through an Indexed Universal Life policy is an ongoing process that requires diligent management and strategic adjustments. By instituting regular reviews, intelligently rebalancing allocations, and staying attuned to life and economic changes, you ensure that your IUL policy is not just a passive component of your financial empire but a robust, dynamic force actively contributing to your wealth-building aspirations.

Incorporating IUL into a Comprehensive Financial Plan

Integrating an Indexed Universal Life (IUL) insurance policy into your financial arsenal can be transformative, serving as both a wealth-building instrument and a robust pillar within your comprehensive financial plan. This process involves understanding how the unique benefits of an IUL synergize with other critical elements like retirement planning, estate management, and overall risk mitigation, all while maintaining balanced portfolio diversification. Here, we explore how you can seamlessly embed an IUL policy into your strategic financial blueprint, aligning it with both your immediate and future aspirations.

1. Synergizing with Retirement Plans

One of the most compelling aspects of an IUL policy is its ability to complement traditional retirement accounts like 401(k)s and IRAs. While these accounts are invaluable, they often come with restrictions on withdrawals, mandatory distribution requirements, and potential tax liabilities upon distribution. An IUL policy can fill these gaps by providing a source of tax-free retirement income through policy loans or withdrawals. This tax-advantaged income stream not only supplements your existing retirement funds but also offers financial flexibility, especially in years when you desire to keep your taxable income lower or when the markets are volatile.

To fully capitalize on this, it is vital to align your IUL policy with your broader retirement goals.

For instance, consider the projected growth of your cash value and how it can offset periods where your market investments may underperform. Regularly revisiting your retirement projections with your financial advisor can ensure that your IUL policy and traditional retirement strategies coalesce into a cohesive retirement plan.

2. Integrating into Estate Planning

An IUL policy can play a pivotal role in estate planning by providing a tax-free death benefit, which can be used to cover estate taxes, ensuring your heirs receive the maximum inheritance possible. Unlike other assets subject to probate, the death benefit from an IUL is generally paid out directly to beneficiaries, offering them immediate liquidity without the burdensome court processes.

Moreover, the cash value within your IUL can be strategically utilized to fund a trust or provide for charitable giving, further aligning with your familial and philanthropic desires. It is prudent to work closely with an estate planning attorney to structure these arrangements, ensuring they are in harmony with the entirety of your estate plan, accounting for both current and future legislative environments.

3. Enhancing Risk Management

Risk management is a cornerstone of any sound financial strategy, and an IUL policy offers distinct advantages here. With its ability to lock in gains while protecting against market downturns, IUL aids in risk mitigation by preserving capital—a critical factor for those nearing retirement or dependent on fixed income streams. The death benefit aspect of an IUL policy further protects against the financial ramifications of an untimely death, offering peace of mind to your family.

Incorporating IUL into your risk management strategy involves assessing your current coverage needs and comparing them to the benefits IUL provides. This might mean resizing other forms of life insurance or liability coverages to realign resources effectively, ensuring you are neither over-insured nor leaving potential financial threats unguarded.

4. **Role in a Diversified Portfolio**

Diversification is the antidote to financial uncertainty and the bedrock of long-term wealth sustainability. An IUL policy introduces a unique asset class into your portfolio, one that is not directly correlated with equities or bonds yet benefits from index-linked growth. This uncorrelated asset quality makes IUL an attractive component, especially when market volatility threatens the stability of traditional asset classes.

To optimally incorporate an IUL policy into your investment strategy, it's essential to conduct periodic reviews of your total asset allocation, ensuring the policy's potential cash value growth is considered alongside your risk tolerance, investment horizon, and specific financial objectives. Collaborating with a financial planner can help identify the proportion of your portfolio that an IUL should represent, ensuring it is both contributory and complementary to the overall strategy.

5. **Aligning with Short- and Long-Term Goals**

Whether your goals include purchasing a second home, funding a child's education, or ensuring a comfortable retirement, an IUL policy offers the adaptability to align with both short- and long-term objectives. The flexibility in accessing the policy's cash value allows for strategic financial maneuvers—borrowing against it for a short-term goal or allowing it to accrue for longer-term aspirations.

In crafting your financial plan, clearly delineate between your short- and long-term goals, assessing how the liquidity and growth potential of an IUL policy can act to meet these objectives. Regular consultations with your financial advisor can adjust these alignments as life circumstances and financial markets evolve.

In conclusion, the multifaceted capabilities of an IUL policy render it a potent element within a comprehensive financial plan. By strategically integrating IUL with retirement, estate, and risk management planning, while ensuring it complements a diversified portfolio and aligns with your actionable goals, you enable your path toward sustainable and scalable wealth creation.

Advanced Wealth Building Tactics with IUL

In the world of sophisticated financial planning, Indexed Universal Life (IUL) insurance stands out as a multi-faceted tool capable of not just preserving wealth, but actively enhancing it for high-net-worth individuals. Leverage, estate planning, and strategic funding are intricately woven into the fabric of IUL's advanced strategies, transforming it into a cornerstone of an astute financial blueprint. To truly maximize its potential, one must dive into high-level tactics that harness its versatile features.

Estate Planning: Securing Generational Wealth

At the heart of IUL's appeal is its efficacy in estate planning—a paramount concern for affluent clients. The tax-free death benefit of an IUL policy makes it an ideal instrument for transferring wealth to heirs without the encumbrance of estate taxes. High-net-worth individuals can position IUL policies within an irrevocable life insurance trust (ILIT), thus excluding the death benefit from their taxable estate. This trust arrangement ensures that their legacy remains protected and distributed according to their wishes, free from the burdens of taxation or probate processes.

Moreover, the flexibility of an IUL allows policyholders to adjust the death benefit as their circumstances change, providing tailor-made solutions for estate liquidity. This liquidity is essential for settling estate taxes and other obligations without having to liquidate other assets hastily, ensuring the continued growth of family wealth.

Funding with Investment Proceeds: Creating a Tax-efficient Environment

For the financially savvy, using investment proceeds to fund IUL premiums is a strategy that merits attention. By pulling from investment gains—especially those that have appreciated significantly—clients can transfer wealth into an IUL policy where it continues to grow on a tax-deferred basis. This move is incredibly advantageous in a high-tax environment where preserving investment gains from the grasp of capital gains taxes is critical.

By reallocating a portion of their investment portfolio into IUL, investors are not only diversifying their holdings but are also leveraging the compound growth potential of the policy's cash value. The cash accumulation within the IUL, linked to market indexes, stands resilient against direct market losses while capturing upside potential—a unique proposition for those managing large portfolios and seeking a balanced risk profile.

Utilizing Policy Loans: Powerful Tools for Wealth Leveraging

IUL policies offer an underutilized yet potent mechanism—policy loans. Unlike traditional loans, borrowing against the accumulated cash value of an IUL does not trigger a taxable event, nor does it come with a rigid repayment schedule. This setup provides an unparalleled degree of financial flexibility, allowing high-net-worth individuals to strategize their capital needs effectively.

Policy loans can serve as a source of liquidity for investment opportunities or emergency funding without disturbing one's cash flow or incurring taxable income. Notable examples include using policy loans to fund new business ventures, capitalize on investment opportunities at attractive valuations, or even as bridge financing for personal undertakings.

Essentially, a policyholder can utilize the borrowed funds to pursue higher yielding investments while the base policy continues its tax-deferred growth. This method can amplify the policyholder's overall net worth if the external returns surpass the policy loan interest rate—a sophisticated form of financial arbitrage.

Integrating with Financial Leverage Strategies

In conjunction with other leverage techniques, IULs can transform into a powerful ally for high-net-worth individuals seeking to optimize their financial position. When strategically paired with instruments like hedge funds or real estate investments, IUL policies can safeguard against downside risks while enjoying the fruits of market advancements. This prudent combination not only shields the individual's wealth but also propels it forward by capturing available market opportunities.

By understanding and utilizing these advanced tactics, the astute investor can transform an Indexed Universal Life policy from a mere insurance instrument to a dynamic component of wealth creation and preservation. The complexities inherent in such strategies necessitate proficient guidance from experienced financial advisors who can tailor these approaches to the client's unique circumstances and goals.

In conclusion, the key to unlocking the full wealth-building potential of IUL lies in its advanced applications—primarily in estate planning, strategic funding, and leveraging policy loans. As with any sophisticated financial tool, thoughtful execution of these tactics requires a discerning eye and adept management, ensuring that the IUL not only safeguards but amplifies one's financial legacy for generations to come.

Chapter 9_Maximizing IUL Tax Benefits

Optimizing Policy Performance through Advanced Allocation Strategies

The allure of Indexed Universal Life (IUL) insurance lies in its unique ability to combine life insurance protection with the potential for cash value growth linked to the performance of market indexes. However, the true essence of an IUL policy's benefits comes from how well you, the policyholder, can optimize its allocation strategies to maximize policy performance. In this subpoint, we will navigate through advanced allocation strategies, focusing on enhancing the potential growth of your IUL policy while maintaining the integrity of its core protections.

Understanding the Mechanics of Index Crediting

Before delving into allocation strategies, it is crucial to have a clear understanding of how index crediting works within an IUL policy. Unlike traditional life insurance, the cash value of an IUL policy grows based on the performance of specific market indexes, such as the S&P 500. The insurance company does not invest directly in the index but rather uses a crediting method, which applies interest to your policy's cash value based on the index's performance. Key components of this are participation rates, caps, and floors, which, when coupled, determine how much credited interest you receive.

Advanced policyholders who are keen on optimization pay particular attention to these components, sophisticatedly analyzing how varying participation rates and caps interact under different economic conditions. Understanding these essentials empowers the policy owner to make informed decisions, aligning the policy with personal financial goals and risk tolerance.

Diversifying Index Options

Once you grasp the mechanics of index crediting, the next step is to diversify your index options. Most IUL policies allow a selection from a variety of index options, each with unique return potential and risk profiles. Advanced policyholders strategically allocate portions of their cash value to different indexes to optimize for both growth and stability.

Instead of betting solely on one index—the S&P 500, for instance—consider spreading your allocations across multiple index options such as international or sector-specific indexes when available. This diversification helps capture a broader spectrum of market gains while mitigating volatility induced by any single index.

The key to success here lies in balancing your allocations in a manner that aligns with your long-term financial objectives and market outlook.

Tactical Allocation Adjustments

Optimal performance in an IUL policy often requires tactical adjustments to allocations based on market conditions. Advanced policyholders routinely assess broader economic indicators and market trends, making calculated changes to index allocations to capitalize on anticipated shifts.

For instance, during a bull market, tactically increasing allocations to high growth potential indexes might accelerate cash value build-up. Conversely, during volatile periods, shifting allocations to more stable or defensive indexes can protect cash value from downside risks while maintaining opportunity for gains. Regularly re-assessing your allocation strategy and being adaptable to changing market conditions can substantially enhance the policy's performance over time.

Utilizing Advanced Policy Features

Many IUL policies come equipped with advanced features such as automatically re-balancing allocations or volatility-controlled indexes. These tools can further enhance policy performance by automatically adjusting allocations to optimize for given market conditions or maintaining a targeted risk profile.

Consider utilizing these features to maintain an effective and efficient allocation strategy that minimizes the time you spend managing your policy while maximizing growth potential. These features—when used strategically—enable your policy to perform well under varying market climates without constant oversight, allowing you to focus on other aspects of your financial strategy.

Customized Allocation Strategy – A Professional Touch

While self-directed strategy is feasible, consulting with a financial advisor or professional experienced in IUL policies can deliver superior outcomes through tailored allocation strategies. Professionals can offer insights into market expectations and devise a strategy that marries index allocation with your overall financial blueprint, taking full advantage of your policy's features and potential.

Such customization ensures that your policy is not just riding market waves sporadically but is instead actively harnessing its nuances to build value effectively.

Optimizing an IUL policy through advanced allocation strategies requires a methodical approach—one that balances personal financial goals with market opportunities. By strategically diversifying index options, tactically adjusting allocations, leveraging policy features, and seeking professional counsel when needed, policyholders can significantly enhance their IUL policy's performance. The discipline and insights gained from these advanced practices not only contribute to the immediate performance of the policy but also set the foundation for enduring financial security and growth. Engaging in these strategies skillfully transforms the potential of an IUL policy from a conventional safety net into a powerful engine for wealth accumulation.

Utilizing IULs to Leverage Policy Loans for Investment Opportunities

Indexed Universal Life (IUL) insurance policies offer a unique and often under-utilized feature: the ability to borrow against the policy's cash value. This feature, known as a policy loan, can be a powerful tool for savvy investors looking to tap into new investment opportunities without having to liquidate other assets or incur tax penalties. In this subpoint, we will delve into how policyholders can leverage policy loans efficiently to seize investment opportunities and maximize their financial strategies.

First, it's important to understand what makes policy loans from an IUL policy particularly advantageous. When you borrow against the cash value of an IUL policy, the loan does not count as a taxable distribution, meaning the funds you receive are tax-free. Additionally, these loans do not require any credit checks, as the cash value in your policy acts as collateral. This can provide flexibility and immediate liquidity, which can be especially beneficial when time-sensitive investment opportunities arise.

One of the intriguing aspects of taking a policy loan is that the interest rates are often more favorable than traditional bank loans or lines of credit. Typically, insurance companies charge a low, fixed rate of interest, or a rate that is tied to the policy's performance index. This can be significantly lower than high-interest credit cards or personal loans, making it a cost-effective option for accessing funds.

Moreover, the beauty of an IUL policy loan is that the cash value continues to grow, even on the amount borrowed. Unlike conventional loans where interest directly affects the principal, the entire cash value continues to earn index-linked interest, which can compound over time. This means that your money is essentially working in two places at once: supporting your new investment without sacrificing the compounding effect within your policy.

So, how can policyholders effectively leverage these features for investment opportunities?

Let's consider a few strategies that exemplify the power of policy loans.

For real estate investors, IUL policy loans can serve as a quick source of funding for property acquisitions. In competitive markets, being able to act swiftly can make the difference between closing a deal and missing out. By using a policy loan to cover down payments or immediate renovation costs, investors can strengthen their purchasing power and expand their portfolios without resorting to costly traditional financing options.

Entrepreneurs may also find policy loans to be instrumental in supporting business expansion or innovation. Starting or expanding a business often requires substantial upfront capital, and a policy loan can provide a ready source of funds, allowing business owners to act on growth opportunities or manage cash flow during lean periods. Because the loan is not recorded as debt in the same way a bank loan might be, it can also leave other lines of credit open.

For those who are inclined towards financial market investments, such as stocks or mutual funds, an IUL policy loan can provide the liquidity needed to enter the market at opportune times. By strategically investing borrowed funds, you could potentially realize returns that outweigh the cost of the loan interest, adding another dimension to your investment strategy. However, it's important to approach this with caution and ensure that risk management practices are in place, as the market's unpredictability can pose significant risks.

While leveraging policy loans for investments holds significant potential, it is crucial to adopt a disciplined approach. It's important for policyholders to recognize that while their policy growth offers a safety net, any outstanding loan balances will typically reduce the death benefit available to beneficiaries. Thus, having a solid repayment plan is essential to mitigate any long-term impact on your policy's overall performance.

In conclusion, leveraging policy loans from an IUL can offer policyholders unprecedented financial flexibility, enabling them to seize investment opportunities that might otherwise be out of reach. Whether funds are used for real estate, business, or financial markets, understanding the mechanics of how these loans operate—and the benefits they afford—is crucial. With prudent management and strategic planning, IUL policy loans can be a linchpin in maximizing your wealth-building potential and achieving your financial goals.

Advanced Tax Planning with IULs

Indexed Universal Life (IUL) insurance is a unique financial tool that offers policyholders not only a life insurance policy but also an investment vehicle with substantial tax benefits. For sophisticated policyholders, the advanced tax planning opportunities within IUL policies can be transformative in managing and growing financial wealth. Understanding these opportunities requires an appreciation of the mechanics behind IUL policies and how they interact with tax laws.

1. Tax-Deferred Growth: A Foundation for Wealth Accumulation

One of the most compelling features of IUL policies is the ability to grow cash value on a tax-deferred basis. Unlike traditional taxable accounts where interest, dividends, and capital gains incur taxes annually, the growth within an IUL policy remains untaxed until the point of withdrawal. This allows your money to compound at an accelerated rate, leveraging what Albert Einstein famously described as "the eighth wonder of the world"compound interest. Tax deferral creates a snowball effect, where policyholders can harness the power of exponential growth without the drag of taxes eroding their gains annually.

2. Harnessing Policy Loans: Unlocking Tax-Free Income

Perhaps one of the most strategic elements of an IUL policy is the ability to borrow against the cash value of the policy through policy loans. These loans are typically not treated as taxable income, provided the policy is structured correctly and does not lapse. This can be a powerful strategy for individuals seeking liquidity without triggering a taxable event. By borrowing against the policy rather than withdrawing, you maintain the tax-deferred growth of the underlying cash value while creating a tax-free income stream when structured properly. Additionally, loans do not have to be repaid during the policyholder's lifetime, as they can be settled against the policy's death benefit, which remains tax-free to beneficiaries.

3. Strategic Withdrawals: Balancing Cash Needs and Tax Efficiency

While loans are one option, withdrawals offer another means of accessing cash from an IUL. Partial withdrawals of the cash value are generally tax-free up to the amount of total premiums paid into the policy—this is the cost basis. Effective tax planning with IUL involves understanding and carefully structuring withdrawals to maximize this tax-free benefit while avoiding creating a Modified Endowment Contract (MEC), which could trigger tax penalties. A deep understanding of MEC guidelines and strategic planning ensures tax efficiency.

4. Avoiding Common Pitfalls: MECs and Lapse Risks

Advanced tax planning with IUL requires an awareness of potential pitfalls that can undermine the tax benefits. Creating a MEC leads to adverse tax treatment, making any loans and withdrawals taxed as income and potentially imposing a 10% penalty if the policyholder is under 59½. Therefore, ensuring your policy is funded and managed appropriately to avoid MEC status is essential for maintaining its tax-advantaged nature.

Additionally, allowing a policy to lapse triggers a taxable event on any outstanding loans exceeding the cost basis. Regularly reviewing your policy with a knowledgeable financial advisor is critical for making informed adjustments that prevent unintended tax consequences.

5. Utilizing IULs for Estate Planning: Passing Wealth Efficiently

For those looking to preserve and pass on wealth, IULs offer the ability to provide tax-free death benefits to beneficiaries. This aspect is invaluable for estate planning, mitigating estate tax liabilities, and ensuring that heirs receive the maximum possible benefit. By structuring the policy with the death benefit in mind, individuals can effectively preserve their legacy while navigating complex estate tax laws.

6. Holistic Financial Strategy: Integration with Other Investments

IUL policies should not be viewed in isolation but rather as a component of a broader financial strategy. By integrating IUL policies with other tax-advantaged accounts, such as Roth IRAs or Health Savings Accounts (HSAs), you can optimize for both tax savings and growth potential. A well-rounded tax planning strategy considers current and future tax brackets, anticipated income streams, and legacy goals, ensuring that IUL policies align with and enhance your overall financial objectives.

In summary, the advanced tax planning strategies available through IUL policies provide policyholders with a dynamic tool for tax-efficient wealth accumulation, income generation, and legacy preservation. By understanding the intricacies of policy loans, withdrawals, and estate planning, individuals can harness these policies to maximize their financial potential while mitigating tax liabilities.

Adapting to Regulatory Changes and Economic Conditions

In an ever-evolving financial landscape, policyholders of Indexed Universal Life (IUL) insurance must remain vigilant and adaptable to thrive. Regulatory changes and economic fluctuations can significantly impact the benefits and functionality of IUL policies. By understanding these dynamics and strategizing effectively, policyholders can safeguard their investments and continue to maximize the potential of their IUL plans.

Understanding Regulatory Changes

Regulatory changes often arise from shifts in government policies, changes in tax laws, or new financial regulations aimed at protecting consumers and ensuring the stability of financial markets. For IUL policyholders, these changes can affect how policies are taxed, the parameters for loans and withdrawals, and even the types of investments insurance companies can make on behalf of policyholders.

For example, adjustments to the tax code that alter how life insurance benefits are taxed can directly affect the strategy for utilizing an IUL policy. Keeping informed about proposed legislative changes and understanding their implications is crucial. Policyholders should collaborate with financial advisors and insurance professionals to anticipate these shifts and make preemptive adjustments to their strategies. This may involve restructuring policy loans, considering additional coverage options, or even re-evaluating the policy's suitability in light of new regulations.

Adapting to Economic Conditions

The economic environment plays a crucial role in the performance of IUL policy. Key economic indicators such as inflation rates, interest rates, and market performance can dictate how the cash value of an IUL policy grows and how quickly it can be accessed.

Inflation and Purchasing Power: Inflation erodes the purchasing power of money, which can affect the cash value build-up in an IUL policy. During periods of high inflation, policyholders should reassess their growth expectations and consider how the policy's growth cap and participation rate are performing relative to inflation. Inflation-linked financial products or riders may offer additional protection, allowing policyholders to maintain the real value of their cash accumulation.

Interest Rate Fluctuations: Interest rates have a direct impact on IUL policies, particularly in terms of the guaranteed interest credited to the policy's cash value. In a rising interest rate environment, the floor protection offered by IULs becomes particularly valuable. Conversely, in a low-interest scenario, policyholders may explore additional premium contributions to benefit from potential market upticks or utilize policy loans when the borrowing costs are advantageous.

Market Performance: Since the cash value of an IUL policy is tied to the performance of a chosen stock market index, economic recessions or bear markets may slow its growth. Understanding the policy's indexing strategy, participation rate, and cap rates is essential. During downturns, it may be prudent to focus on the policy's downside protection feature, which protects the principal in volatile times. In anticipation of market shifts, consider re-evaluating the chosen index or diversifying among multiple indices to mitigate risks and seek optimal growth opportunities.

Proactive Strategies for Change

To successfully navigate these changes, proactive planning is key. Regular policy reviews and performance assessments are crucial to ensure that the IUL policy aligns with current financial goals and adapts to any legislative or economic changes.

1. **Engage with Financial Professionals:** Regular consultations with a knowledgeable financial advisor or insurance specialist can provide insights and guidance on any necessary adjustments to your IUL policy. They can assist in understanding upcoming regulatory impacts and exploring new riders or features that may be beneficial.

2. **Policy Flexibility Utilization:** Leverage the inherent flexibility of IUL policies, such as adjustable premiums and flexible death benefits, to respond effectively to both regulatory and economic changes. For instance, increasing or decreasing policy premiums can optimize cash value growth or alleviate financial strain during economic downturns.

3. **Continual Education:** Staying informed through webinars, seminars, and industry publications can keep policyholders up to date with the latest changes in legislation and market trends. Understanding these developments

empowers informed decision-making and strategic adjustments.

By being attentive to these dynamic elements and employing strategic foresight, policyholders can continue to harness the benefits of IUL policies to fortify their financial portfolios. With careful planning and timely adaptation, IUL owners can turn potential regulatory and economic challenges into opportunities for growth and financial security.

Utilizing IULs in Retirement Planning

When it comes to retirement planning, traditional vehicles such as 401(k)s, IRAs, and Roth IRAs often dominate the conversation. However, Indexed Universal Life (IUL) insurance has emerged as a powerful complementary tool, offering unique advantages that can enhance a retirement strategy. Recognizing the potential of IULs in retirement planning involves understanding their ability to provide not only death benefits but also tax-advantaged income streams, growth potential tied to market indices, and downside protection.

Firstly, one of the most compelling features of an IUL policy in the context of retirement planning is its ability to generate tax-free income. Unlike traditional retirement accounts, which often involve paying taxes upon withdrawal, IUL allows policyholders to access the cash value via policy loans. These loans are tax-free under current federal tax guidelines, provided the policy remains in force. This feature can significantly enhance the net income received during retirement and offers a predictable income stream that isn't vulnerable to the fluctuations of tax legislation changes.

Moreover, IULs provide policyholders with the advantage of tax-deferred growth. The cash value of an IUL accrues interest linked to specific market indexes, such as the S&P 500, but unlike direct market investments, this growth is not subject to annual taxation. This tax-deferred compounding can lead to substantial growth over the life of the policy, amplifying the amount available for retirement income. It allows policyholders to benefit from market upswings while mitigating the taxation impact during the accumulation phase.

Another critical aspect of utilizing IULs in retirement planning is their inherent flexibility. Life can be unpredictable, and the financial goals for retirement can shift due to various life events. IULs offer adaptability by allowing policyholders to adjust premium payments and death benefit amounts to suit changing needs. This flexibility ensures that the policy can evolve with a policyholder's financial situation, providing security and peace of mind as retirement approaches.

The contractually guaranteed downside protection provided by IULs cannot be understated. Market volatility is a significant concern for individuals nearing or in retirement. Traditional stock market investments expose retirement savings to substantial risks during downturns. In contrast, IULs safeguard the accumulated cash value from market losses, ensuring that a policyholder's nest egg remains intact even during economic tumult. This protective feature is grounded in the policy's structure, where cash values are linked to an index but not directly invested in the stock market.

Furthermore, leveraging IULs for retirement also means benefiting from the policy's death benefit as a legacy planning tool. Although the primary focus often lies on cash value for income, the death benefit of an IUL can serve as a crucial component of estate planning. After all, what remains after borrowing from the cash value can transfer to heirs tax-free. For many, this means offering beneficiaries a financial cushion or legacy while simultaneously drawing down retirement income.

Integrating an IUL policy into a comprehensive retirement strategy also supports hedging against inflation. As the cost of living rises over time, ensuring that retirement income is appreciated accordingly is vital. The growth component of an IUL, which is potentially far superior to the interest earned in savings accounts or some bonds, coupled with no exposure to direct market losses, positions it as an effective inflation buffer.

Lastly, IUL policies do not have the required minimum distributions (RMDs) like some traditional retirement accounts. This lack of RMDs provides retirees with greater control over how and when they access their funds, offering flexibility that aligns better with the individual's overall retirement strategy and financial needs as they evolve over time.

In conclusion, leveraging Indexed Universal Life insurance as a component of retirement planning entails harnessing its tax-free income generation capabilities, market-linked growth potential, downside protection, and flexibility. By embedding an IUL policy into a broader retirement plan, policyholders can safeguard themselves against market volatility, ensure a stream of tax-advantaged income, and lay a solid foundation for passing wealth to the next generation. As always, it's advisable for individuals to consult with a financial advisor to tailor an IUL strategy that aligns with their specific financial goals and retirement needs, ensuring that the policy maximizes their wealth-building potential while addressing unique retirement objectives.

Strategic Use of IULs in Business Succession Planning

In the intricate landscape of business succession planning, smart financial instruments play a pivotal role in ensuring the seamless transition of ownership and leadership. Indexed Universal Life (IUL) insurance policies emerge as a powerful asset in this domain, offering unique benefits that can be strategically leveraged to achieve a smooth and efficient succession process. This section delves into how IUL policies can be maximized within the framework of business succession planning, ensuring the financial stability and longevity of the business as well as the fulfillment of the owner's legacy vision.

Harnessing IULs for Liquidity Needs

One of the primary considerations in business succession is ensuring that liquidity is available to address various financial obligations that may arise during the transition. Taxes related to estate and inheritance can be particularly burdensome, potentially forcing a business to liquidate key assets if proper planning isn't in place. IUL policies address these needs by providing a tax-free death benefit that beneficiaries can use to cover estate taxes, professional fees, and other immediate financial obligations. This allows the business itself to remain intact and operational, shielding it from the disruptions that occur when critical assets must be sold to meet liquidity demands.

Facilitating Buy-Sell Agreements

A buy-sell agreement is a fundamental element of succession planning, outlining how ownership interests will be transferred and valued. IUL policies are an excellent funding method for these agreements, particularly in closely held businesses. Business partners can utilize the cash value accumulation feature of an IUL to finance the buyout of shares from retiring or deceased partners. The policy's death benefit can also provide the necessary funds to purchase the departing partner's interest, facilitating a smooth transition without straining the business's operational funds. Additionally, the growth potential linked to market indices ensures that the policy's cash value is appreciated over time, providing an inflation-adjusted resource for future buyouts.

Retaining Key Employees

The retention of key employees is often critical during succession processes, as these individuals typically hold essential knowledge and skills crucial for maintaining business continuity. An IUL policy can be used as a golden handcuff strategy, offering executives or valued employees a supplemental retirement plan. The policy can be structured to provide tax-free income in retirement as long as the employee remains with the company until a specified milestone. This fosters loyalty and reduces the risk of losing key personnel at a time when their contribution to the organization's stability and growth is most needed.

Legacy Planning and Long-Term Financial Security

For business owners, the preservation of their legacy is often as integral as the financial planning aspect of succession. IUL policies offer a dual benefit in this regard. Firstly, the tax-free death benefit ensures that a legacy is preserved through the financial security it imparts to the successors. Secondly, the accumulated cash value can be allocated toward funding charitable endeavors or ensuring the business operates along the vision of its founding principles. This ensures that the business owner's entrepreneurial spirit and values continue to guide the organization even after their tenure.

Tax Optimization

Succession planning inherently involves meticulous tax strategizing, given the potential tax implications connected with transferring business ownership. IUL policies play a crucial role, as the policy's proceeds are generally exempt from income and estate taxes when properly structured. This advantage allows for a significant reduction in the taxable estate value. Moreover, the capacity to borrow against the cash value of an IUL without triggering tax consequences offers additional financial flexibility in managing business finances, thus optimizing the tax position of both the owner and the successors.

In summary, the strategic incorporation of Indexed Universal Life insurance policies within business succession planning serves as a multifaceted tool, harmonizing the objectives of legacy preservation, financial security, and strategic tax planning. By addressing liquidity needs, facilitating buy-sell agreements, retaining key employees, and securing long-term tax optimization, IULs provide a comprehensive solution that supports a smooth transition and perpetuates business success and stability. Therefore, business owners who are contemplating or engaging in succession planning should consider the integrative and enduring advantages that IUL policies can offer within this vital framework.

Chapter 10: Strategic Benefits of IUL for Business Owners

Introduction to IUL Benefits for Business Owners

In the rapidly evolving landscape of modern business, finding financial instruments that offer both growth potential and security is akin to striking gold. Indexed Universal Life (IUL) insurance serves as one such tool, providing a myriad of benefits to business owners and entrepreneurs navigating the complexities of today's economic environment. Unlike traditional investment avenues, IUL policies offer unique advantages tailored to meet the diverse needs of business-minded individuals seeking to protect and grow their wealth while planning for the future.

Tax-Advantaged Growth and Wealth Preservation

One of the most compelling features of IUL policies is their tax-advantaged growth potential. As business owners, understanding the ramifications of tax liabilities on profit margins and cash flow is essential. With IUL, the cash value grows tax-deferred, allowing business owners to accumulate wealth without the immediate tax burdens associated with more conventional investments. This aspect of an IUL is particularly beneficial for high-income business owners who are constantly seeking ways to optimize tax efficiency while maximizing the reinvestment potential of their profits.

Moreover, the policy's growth is linked to market indexes, giving you the opportunity to benefit from market upswings while enjoying protection against downturns. This means that your invested premiums can garner attractive returns during positive market performance, yet the structure of the policy ensures that they won't suffer losses when the market takes a dip. This balanced risk-reward equation is particularly advantageous for entrepreneurs who are often already exposed to financial risks in their ventures.

Flexibility in Premium and Coverage Adjustments

Flexibility is at the heart of what makes IUL policies attractive for business owners. Running a business is a dynamic endeavor, and the ability to adjust your financial commitments in response to changing circumstances is invaluable. IULs typically allow for flexible premium payments, meaning you have the latitude to adjust the amount you contribute to the policy over time, as business cycles fluctuate. During periods of growth, you might opt to increase your premiums to accelerate the cash value growth within the policy. Conversely, in tighter financial times, you may reduce your

251

premium payments without sacrificing your policy's viability.

Additionally, the flexibility to adjust death benefits can be a strategic tool in business planning. Many business owners use these policies for key-person insurance or as part of their succession strategy. As the business evolves, so too can the coverage need, and IUL's adaptability allows you to modify the policy to align with current business valuations or future projections.

Access to Policy Loans for Business Needs

For entrepreneurs, liquidity is king. The ability to access funds when opportunities arise, or challenges emerge can be pivotal to business success. IUL policies enable policyholders to take loans against their accumulated cash value, providing an avenue to access significant capital without the need for traditional borrowing methods that could impact credit ratings or require extensive collateral.

Importantly, these policy loans are generally tax-free, provided the policy remains in force, and they can be paid back on flexible terms set by the policyholder. This feature can be strategically utilized for business expansion, to bridge cash flow gaps, or even to capitalize on unexpected opportunities that require immediate funding. Furthermore, during succession planning, these funds can aid in the executing buy-sell agreements, ensuring that the business transitions smoothly to the next generation or to new ownership without the typical financial strain associated with such transitions.

Protection Against Business Risks

Apart from the growth and tax advantages, IULs offer intrinsic protection through the policy's death benefit. This feature can play a crucial role in protecting your business against the financial fallout associated with the loss of a key business partner or owner. The death benefit can provide an infusion of capital to cover ongoing obligations, stabilizing the company in what would otherwise be a tumultuous period.

In sum, IUL policies present a multi-faceted financial tool specifically advantageous for business owners. They offer a strategic combination of tax-advantaged growth, flexible structuring, access to capital, and robust protection mechanisms. In an environment where financial agility can dictate business survival and expansion, IUL insurance serves not just as a mere policy but as a strategic component of long-term business planning and wealth management. By embedding an IUL policy within your business's financial strategy, you are positioning yourself to not only thrive in the present but also secure your enterprise's future under a canopy of protection and opportunity.

Leveraging IUL for Business Expansion

Leveraging an Indexed Universal Life (IUL) policy for business expansion is a compelling strategy that marries insurance and investment advantages to support business growth. Beyond its primary role as a life insurance policy, IUL serves as a financial reservoir that smart entrepreneurs can tap into for fueling business aspirations. By comprehending and utilizing the cash value accumulation feature inherent to IULs, business owners can strategically enhance their ventures without incurring the burdens commonly associated with traditional financing methods.

The first step to leveraging IUL for business expansion lies in understanding the distinct mechanics of cash value growth. An IUL policy credits interest to the cash value based on the performance of a chosen market index, such as the S&P 500, yet it provides a safety net by guaranteeing a minimum return, typically around 0-2%, ensuring that your principal remains protected even in downturns. This combination of growth potential and risk mitigation makes IUL a robust tool for accumulating capital over time. For entrepreneurs, this translates to having a financial pool that aligns with market upswings, ready to be accessed when business opportunities arise.

One of the key advantages of using an IUL policy for business needs is the ability to take policy loans against the accumulated cash value. Unlike traditional business loans, these policy loans typically don't require a credit check or collateral – the cash value serves as the collateral itself. Moreover, since you are essentially borrowing from yourself, the repayment terms are exceptionally flexible. For a business owner, this means accessing capital without the prolonged and sometimes arduous process of securing a loan from external financial institutions. You can deploy these funds to finance new projects, invest in additional resources, or even manage cash flow during lean periods.

The tax-advantaged nature of an IUL policy further enhances its appeal. When borrowing against the policy's cash value, the loan is not considered taxable income. This creates a tax-efficient strategy for financing business endeavors. Additionally, because the policy grows on a tax-deferred basis, the interest credited to the cash value does not incur immediate taxes, allowing the business owner to maximize growth potential without immediate tax liabilities.

Moreover, leveraging an IUL for business expansion can also complement succession planning strategies. As business owners look to the future, ensuring a smooth transition of leadership is paramount. The cash value of an IUL can be harnessed to buy out the interests of departing partners or to redistribute shares to align with strategic succession plans. This ensures continuity and stability, which are critical components of a successful succession strategy.

Beyond loans, the IUL policy's death benefit can serve as a strategic tool for business continuity. Upon the death of the insured, the death benefit can be designated to cover outstanding debts, ensuring the business remains solvent and operational for future generations. This aspect of the IUL policy confers peace of mind, knowing that your business will have the necessary liquidity to navigate the challenges that come with the absence of a key leader.

In practice, an entrepreneur must approach the idea of using an IUL policy judiciously. It is crucial to work with a financial advisor who specializes in IUL policies to design a strategy that aligns with your specific business goals. This involves structuring the policy and its premiums to facilitate optimum growth of cash value over time while ensuring that the business's liquidity needs can be met efficiently.

Properly managing an IUL requires a careful balance between maximizing the cash value growth and maintaining the policy's viability with regular premium payments.

In conclusion, an IUL policy provides a multifaceted tool that business owners can leverage to achieve a variety of financial goals. By tapping into the policy's cash value, entrepreneurs can fund business expansions without the typical drawbacks of external financing, such as dilutive equity or restrictive debt covenants. The combination of growth potential, tax advantages, and strategic flexibility makes IUL an attractive option for those looking to elevate their business ventures while maintaining financial security. As with any financial strategy, it behooves business owners to thoroughly analyze how an IUL can fit into their broader expansion plans, ensuring that they harness its benefits to propel their businesses to new heights while safeguarding their long-term financial health.

IUL in Succession Planning

Understanding the Role of IUL in Succession Planning

As a business owner or entrepreneur, preparing for the seamless transition of your enterprise to the next generation or new leadership is crucial for maintaining its long-term success. Indexed Universal Life (IUL) insurance can be a pivotal tool in crafting a succession plan that not only facilitates an orderly transition but also maximizes financial efficiency and tax advantages.

Succession planning involves more than just identifying who will take over the business. It requires careful consideration of financial implications, tax consequences, and aligning the transfer with your overall wealth management goals. IUL insurance offers a unique blend of benefits that can address these concerns effectively.

At its core, an IUL policy is a life insurance product that provides a death benefit, which can serve as a financial safety net for the business. This is critical in ensuring that your company has the liquidity needed to survive the transition phase without the disruption of its operations. The death benefit can provide the necessary funds to cover costs associated with transferring ownership, such as paying off outstanding business debts, covering estate taxes, or buying out other stakeholders.

Utilizing Cash Value for Buy-Sell Agreements

A key component of effective succession planning is the establishment of a buy-sell agreement. These agreements ensure that the transition of business ownership happens according to predetermined terms. They are essentially contracts that dictate how a business partner's shares will be reassigned upon a triggering event, like retirement, disability, or death.

IUL policies can be structured to accumulate cash value, which can be accessed to fund a buy-sell agreement. Over time, as you pay premiums, the policy accumulates cash value, which grows based on the performance of a chosen market index, offering the potential for higher growth compared to traditional whole life insurance products. This cash value can be borrowed against or withdrawn to facilitate the buyout of an owner's share, providing a ready source of funding without the need to liquidate other business assets or secure external financing.

Tax Advantaged Benefits

One of the most compelling aspects of using IUL in succession planning is the tax advantages it offers. The death benefit provided by an IUL policy is generally tax-free, which is a significant advantage when considering estate taxes and the financial impact they can have on the transfer of business ownership. Additionally, the cash value growth in an IUL policy is tax-deferred, which allows for strategic use of these funds at a time when they are most needed in the succession planning process.

Moreover, the ability to take out tax-free loans against the policy's cash value can provide liquidity to pay potential capital gains taxes or other liabilities that arise during the ownership transfer. This ensures that the transition does not force the business into a cash-strapped situation, which is common when taxes consume a significant portion of available liquid assets.

Stability and Flexibility

The guarantee of a death benefit in an IUL policy provides a layer of stability that is reassuring to the outgoing owner, incoming successors, and stakeholders. It signals financial health and readiness for change, enhancing stakeholder confidence during the transition phase. Furthermore, IUL offers flexibility in premium payments and death benefit options, allowing it to be fine-tuned to match the specific needs and cash flow capabilities of the business.

The flexible nature of IUL policies allows business owners to adjust coverage amounts and premium payments, catering to the fluctuating financial states often experienced by thriving businesses. These adjustments can be crucial in adapting to changes in the business environment or shifts in succession timelines.

Real-World Application

An example of IUL in succession planning involves a family-owned business preparing for generational transition. By incorporating an IUL policy, the business owner ensures his successors have immediate access to funds required for estate tax payments and also provides liquidity to purchase shares from non-family stakeholders, thus keeping the control within the family.

Overall, the incorporation of IUL insurance into succession planning offers business owners a robust, tax-advantaged, and flexible mechanism to ensure the longevity and resilience of their enterprise. By planning ahead with an IUL policy, business owners and entrepreneurs can preserve and extend their legacy, secure in the knowledge that they have taken proactive steps to fortify their business's future.

Tax Advantages Specific to Business Owners

When it comes to financial strategies for business owners, leveraging the tax advantages of Indexed Universal Life (IUL) insurance can be a game-changer. IUL policies offer distinct benefits that cater to the unique financial needs of entrepreneurs, providing not only a robust safety net but also a powerful tool for tax-advantaged wealth accumulation. Let us delve into the specifics of how business owners can harness these advantages to optimize their financial strategy.

1. **Tax-Free Death Benefit:** One of the primary tax advantages of an IUL policy is the ability to receive a tax-free death benefit. For business owners, this can serve several critical functions. Upon the death of the policyholder, the beneficiaries receive the death benefit without the burden of federal income tax. This means that if a business owner structures their IUL policy as part of a buy-sell agreement, this benefit can be seamlessly transferred to fund the purchase of shares in the business, ensuring a smooth transition in ownership without the additional tax

burden. It also allows for the continuity of the business by providing essential liquidity to cover unforeseen expenses, thus securing the business's future.

2. **Tax-Deferred Growth:** The cash value component of an IUL gains interest tied to a market index, and it grows on a tax-deferred basis. This means that as the cash value increases, business owners do not have to pay taxes on the gains each year, unlike other financial instruments. This allows the cash value to compound over time without yearly taxable events, potentially leading to significant accumulation over the years. For business owners looking to fund future expansions or investments without tapping into company profits, this tax-advantaged growth is invaluable.

3. **Access to Tax-Free Loans:** Another significant tax advantage of IUL policies is the ability to take loans against the accumulated cash value without triggering a taxable event. For business owners, this means access to capital that can be used for various business needs such as expansion, capital improvements, or even bridging cash flow gaps, without affecting their cash reserves or impacting their tax liability. By

borrowing against the policy, business owners can strategically leverage these funds while keeping the policy intact and retaining their equity positions elsewhere.

4. **Premium Financing Opportunities:** Business owners often have the opportunity to utilize premium financing to pay for the IUL policy. This involves borrowing money to pay the premiums and using the policy's cash value and death benefit as collateral. This strategy can dramatically enhance the earning potential of the business's cash flow, as the funds that would have otherwise been earmarked for premium payments can be reinvested into the business to generate potentially higher returns. This creates a tax-efficient cycle of wealth generation and policy funding.

5. **Tax Optimization in Business Succession Planning:** In the realm of succession planning, an IUL policy can play a pivotal role in minimizing tax implications during the transfer of business ownership. Whether passing the business to heirs or selling to partners, the cash value and death benefits can be strategically utilized to offset estate taxes and provide liquidity

during the transition phase. This ensures that the succession plan is financially viable and not encumbered by cumbersome tax-related expenses.

6. **Employee Benefit Programs:** An often-overlooked tax advantage for business owners is the use of IUL policies as part of a selective executive compensation package. Offering top-performing employees a supplemental executive retirement plan (SERP) funded by an IUL policy can be a highly attractive benefit, helping to retain key personnel while providing them with tax-advantaged retirement income. The premiums paid by the business can often be structured in a way that is tax-deductible, depending on the setup of the plan, providing further tax relief to the employer.

In conclusion, the tax advantages of IUL policies create multifaceted opportunities for business owners, providing an effective conduit for wealth preservation and growth. By incorporating an IUL policy into their financial strategy, entrepreneurs can leverage these tax benefits to ensure business sustainability, optimize cash flow, and enhance their long-term financial security. As with any complex financial tool, it is essential for business owners to consult with knowledgeable financial advisors to tailor an IUL strategy that aligns with their unique business goals and tax considerations.

Case Studies of Successful Business Owners Using IUL

Indexed Universal Life (IUL) insurance has emerged as a powerful financial tool for business owners, offering a unique combination of flexibility, growth potential, and protection. To illustrate its efficacy, let's explore several case studies where successful entrepreneurs have harnessed the potential of IUL to achieve remarkable financial outcomes.

Case Study 1: The Tech Entrepreneur's Expansion Strategy

John, a tech entrepreneur, founded a dynamic software firm that quickly gained traction. As the business grew, John sought funding pathways that aligned with his risk-aversion preferences and long-term goals. An IUL policy presented an attractive option: it not only ensured tax-deferred growth of cash value but also provided a death benefit, adding a layer of financial security for his family.

John leveraged the cash value of his IUL policy to finance the company's expansion into emerging markets. By using the loan provisions of his IUL, he was able to access necessary funds without incurring taxes that typically accompany the withdrawal of conventional investment assets. Moreover, his policy's cash value continued to grow, linked to market indexes, yet sheltered from market volatility due to built-in downside protection features.

The expansion was a success, substantially increasing the company's revenue streams. The IUL strategy provided John with financing flexibility, reduced tax burdens, and ensured that his heirs would receive the policy's death benefit, safeguarding their financial future regardless of business outcomes.

Case Study 2: The Family-Owned Business Succession Plan

Samantha owned a successful family-run restaurant chain. Her primary goal was to smoothly transition ownership to her children without disrupting operations or family harmony. Recognizing the complexities involved in business transfer, Samantha consulted her financial planner, who recommended utilizing an IUL policy as a strategic part of the succession plan.

By purchasing IUL policies for each of her children, Samantha facilitated a tax-advantaged way to ensure liquidity when the time came to transfer ownership—thus avoiding potential financial strain on the business. As the policies accrued cash value, they provided a financial cushion, enabling the children to handle operational or unforeseen expenses without tapping into business accounts.

The IUL policies served not only as structured financial support during the transition but also secured a legacy of financial responsibility and security, ensuring the restaurant chain's continued success across generations.

Case Study 3: The Real Estate Mogul's Legacy Building

David, a real estate investor with an expansive portfolio, was acutely aware of the need for strategic wealth preservation and tax minimization. He was introduced to IUL as an innovative vehicle for achieving these goals. Unlike many traditional investments, IUL enabled David to accumulate wealth tax-deferred while enjoying the potential for market-based growth with downside protection.

David utilized the cash value growth of his IUL to fund new property acquisitions, strategically enhancing his real estate holdings without liquidating existing assets or incurring capital gains taxes. Furthermore, the IUL provided a built-in estate planning tool, enabling David to pass along a substantial tax-free death benefit to his heirs, effectively preserving generational wealth.

This approach safeguarded his assets from estate taxes and litigation risks, ensuring that the family could retain and benefit from his meticulously built real estate empire.

Case Study 4: The Creative Agency's Credit Line Alternative

Michelle ran a successful creative agency that experienced seasonal cash flow fluctuations. Traditionally, she relied on credit lines to manage these variations, often facing high interest and fees. Transitioning to an IUL policy as a financial management tool offered Michelle an innovative solution.

By building up the cash value of her IUL, she established an internal reserve that could be accessed whenever the agency needed short-term liquidity. This practice not only mitigated her reliance on costly external credit but also allowed earnings to continue growing within the policy, enhancing long-term financial stability.

When market downturns impacted client spending, the built-in downside protection of her IUL ensured the cash value did not diminish, allowing Michelle to maintain operational stability and capitalize on new opportunities as market conditions improved.

These case studies underscore the versatile applications of IUL for business owners across various industries. Whether used for expansion, succession planning, asset backing, or liquidity management, IUL policies offer a robust, flexible framework that aligns with diverse business objectives. By skillfully integrating IUL into their strategic financial planning, these business leaders effectively leveraged its unique advantages to secure their enterprises, protect their families, and build enduring legacies.

Best Practices and Practical Tips for Implementing IUL Strategies

Implementing Indexed Universal Life (IUL) insurance strategies is an astute move for business owners and entrepreneurs seeking to leverage tax-advantaged wealth-building opportunities. However, to maximize the benefits that IUL policies offer, one must approach them with a strategic mindset, combining best practices with practical insights tailored to unique needs. Below, I delve into the essential strategies and practical tips to effectively capitalize on IUL policies for business success.

1. Define Your Objectives Clearly

Before diving into any IUL strategy, it's crucial to have a thorough understanding of your financial goals. Whether it's funding business expansion, succession planning, or securing a steady income stream for retirement, clearly defined objectives will guide your decisions. As a business owner, consider how an IUL policy can integrate with your broader financial and strategic plans. This clarity ensures you're utilizing the policy to support both your personal and professional aspirations.

2. **Understand Policy Features and Options**

Each IUL policy may come with different features, options, and flexibility. It's essential to understand terms such as cash value growth, various death benefit options, index crediting methods, and so forth. Familiarize yourself with the choices that affect the policy's performance, like choosing the right index or selecting between fixed and variable interest rate strategies. Knowledge of these aspects will empower you to tailor your policy to optimize benefits.

3. **Leverage Tax Advantages Smartly**

One of the greatest draws of IUL policies is their tax-deferred growth. Use this to your advantage by allowing investments to compound overtime without the immediate burden of taxes. Properly structured, loans against the cash value of an IUL can be tax-free as they are not considered distributions. This unique feature can be a powerful tool for managing company cash flow or funding personal ventures without increasing taxable income.

4. **Implementing a Diversification Strategy**

Just as you would in traditional investing, diversification within your IUL policy can be beneficial. By allocating your cash value across different indices or a mixture of index and fixed account options, you can mitigate risk and capitalize on market opportunities. This diversification helps reduce exposure to any single market downturn and optimizes growth potential from various economic conditions.

5. Adopt a Long-Term Perspective

IUL policies are particularly suited for long-term wealth accumulation. Their benefits become more profound over time as cash value growth compounds and tax advantages accrue. Business owners should resist the temptation for short-term gains and instead focus on the enduring benefits of policy growth and stability for future business and personal financial needs.

6. Stay Agile and Rebalance Periodically

Economic conditions and personal business circumstances can change. Therefore, it's vital to periodically review and adjust your IUL policy to ensure it aligns with both current and future financial goals. This may involve reallocating resources within the policy or adjusting premiums. Staying agile allows policyholders to react effectively to new opportunities or challenges as they arise.

7. Collaboration with Financial Experts

While business owners are experts in their field, the intricacies of life insurance and financial planning require specific expertise. Engage with seasoned financial advisors or tax professionals who can provide insights tailored to your business structure and personal financial circumstances. Their guidance will be invaluable in navigating complex IUL strategies and maximizing their potential.

8. Plan for Succession Early

An IUL policy can be effectively employed as a tool for business succession planning. By ensuring that there is liquidity in the form of a policy's death benefit, business owners can facilitate a smooth transition of ownership. This is particularly crucial for family businesses or partnerships, where such tools can provide cash to settle estate taxes, buy out stakes, or finance new leadership.

9. Educating Key Stakeholders

Implementing an IUL strategy within your business may involve key stakeholders, such as family members, business partners, or employees. Educate them on the benefits and mechanics of the policy to ensure alignment and support. This can foster a collective commitment to shared financial goals and clearer succession or expansion planning.

10. Monitor Competitive Offerings and Innovations

The financial landscape and insurance products evolve over time. Stay informed about new developments and offerings in the IUL market. Innovations or competitive features from providers could enhance the effectiveness of your strategy or present new opportunities for growth.

Implementing these best practices and practical tips will ensure that business owners fully harness the power of IUL policies, turning them into a cornerstone for achieving both personal and business financial success.

Chapter 11: The Future of Indexed Universal Life

Analyzing Current Trends in the IUL Market

The Indexed Universal Life (IUL) insurance market has been historically dynamic, responding to shifts in regulatory landscapes, economic conditions, and evolving consumer needs. As we look to the future, analyzing current trends in the IUL market reveals significant shifts that are poised to impact how these policies are designed, sold, and utilized by policyholders.

One of the most salient trends in the IUL market is the increasing consumer interest in flexible and customizable financial products. Modern investors are more informed and demand financial tools that can be tailored to their specific needs. IUL policies have responded to this demand by enhancing the degree of customization available to policyholders. Insurers now offer a variety of riders and features that allow policyholders to adjust coverage amounts, switch between indexing strategies, and even change death benefit options to suit their current life circumstances.

This heightened demand for customization is accompanied by a considerable push for greater transparency. Consumers, armed with vast amounts of information at their fingertips, desire clarity in how their policies work, the fees involved, and how returns are calculated. Insurance companies have responded by simplifying policy documents and ensuring that clients understand the mechanics of their IUL policy, especially how the cash value is tied to underlying indices like the S&P 500. Transparency in fee structures and indexing methodologies is not simply the best practice; it is a competitive advantage.

Technological advancements are another driving force shaping the IUL market. The digital revolution has permeated every aspect of the insurance industry, and IUL is no exception. Digital platforms are enhancing the policyholder experience by making it possible to track the performance of an IUL policy in real time. This technological shift is influencing how insurance agents interact with clients, offering digital advisory services and virtual consultations that are both convenient and efficient. Moreover, the advent of AI and big data analytics is helping insurers better forecast risks and optimize policy designs, ensuring that IUL products remain competitive and attractive.

Another notable trend is the increasing awareness and incorporation of environmental, social, and governance (ESG) factors in investment strategies, including within the insurance industry. Policyholders are increasingly interested in how their funds are invested, seeking alignment with personal values without sacrificing performance. Insurers are responding by offering IUL products that track ESG-compliant indices, balancing social responsibility with traditional investment objectives. This shift could redefine what consumers expect from IUL policies, blending wealth-building with ethical investment considerations.

The regulatory environment is also influencing IUL trends. Recent tax law changes and ongoing discussions regarding the tax treatment of life insurance products could have far-reaching effects. As governments grapple with fiscal challenges, the tax advantages traditionally afforded to IUL policyholders may face scrutiny or adjustments. Insurers and policyholders alike must stay vigilant, adapting strategies to maintain tax efficiency that makes IUL an attractive option for wealth-building.

Additionally, demographic changes are shifting the landscape of the IUL market. As Baby Boomers retire, there is an increasing focus on distribution strategies and preserving wealth during retirement. IUL policies are adapting to these demographic shifts by offering attractive loan provisions and withdrawal strategies to generate tax-free retirement income. Simultaneously, younger generations like

Millennials and Gen Z, who exhibit different financial behaviors and risk tolerances, are entering the market. These cohorts are more inclined toward digital experiences and socially responsible investments, driving changes in how IUL policies are marketed and implemented.

Lastly, the economic climate plays an essential role in shaping the IUL market. In a world marked by economic uncertainty and fluctuating market conditions, the appeal of IUL's downside protection grows stronger. Policyholders are increasingly appreciative of the shield against market losses, as guaranteed components protect principal investments in volatile times. This feature, coupled with potential for growth, ensures that IUL remains an attractive proposition for risk-averse individuals seeking to build wealth over the long term.

In conclusion, the current trends in the IUL market highlight an exciting intersection of personalization, technology, social responsibility, regulatory influence, and demographic diversity. As the market evolves, staying attuned to these trends will be crucial for insurance companies and policyholders alike, ensuring that IUL remains a leading option for those seeking both protection and growth in their financial planning endeavors.

Technological Innovations Enhancing IUL Policies

In recent years, technology has become a catalyst for transformation across the financial sector, and Indexed Universal Life (IUL) insurance is no exception. As a wealth-building tool, IUL policies have historically been lauded for their flexibility, tax advantages, and potential for growth. However, like any financial instrument, they must evolve to meet the needs of modern consumers. Technological innovations are not only enhancing the design and execution of these policies but are also redefining the ways in which policyholders interact with and benefit from them.

One of the most significant technological advancements impacting IUL policies is the integration of artificial intelligence (AI) and data analytics. Insurers are harnessing the power of AI to tailor IUL policies to individual clients more precisely than ever before. By analyzing vast amounts of consumer data, including spending habits, investment preferences, and risk tolerance, insurers can craft personalized policies that align closely with a client's financial goals. This level of customization is not only improving customer satisfaction but is also contributing to better risk assessment and pricing models, providing clients with more competitive premium rates.

Furthermore, predictive analytics are enhancing the way insurers forecast potential policy outcomes. These sophisticated analytical tools can simulate various market scenarios, allowing policyholders to understand potential growth trajectories under different conditions. By leveraging historical data and advanced algorithms, insurers offer clients a clearer picture of how their policy's cash value might evolve in relation to market indexes like the S&P 500. This transparency empowers policyholders with the foresight needed for informed decision-making, ultimately making IUL policies more attractive to savvy investors.

The digital transformation extends beyond policy design into the realm of customer service and engagement. The emergence of self-service platforms and mobile applications is reshaping policyholder experience. These digital tools allow clients to access their policy information, track cash value growth, and manage their account settings from the comfort of their homes. The convenience of on-demand access is supplemented by digital assistant features, which offer real-time insights and answers to common policy-related queries. This self-guided approach not only enhances customer satisfaction but also reduces administrative burdens on insurers, allowing them to allocate resources more effectively.

Blockchain technology is another technological innovation beginning to make waves in the IUL insurance arena. By offering an immutable and transparent ledger for transactions, blockchain facilitates streamlined and secure policy administration. It holds the potential to automate numerous processes, from underwriting to claims settlement, significantly reducing processing times and operating costs. Blockchain's transparency also fosters trust among policyholders, assuring them of the integrity and accuracy of their transactions.

Insurance technology, or Insurtech, startups are playing a pivotal role in driving innovation within the IUL market. These disruptive entities are challenging traditional insurance models by introducing platform-based solutions that prioritize ease of use, transparency, and agility. Many of these startups are partnering with established insurers to integrate innovative features that enhance policy offerings and simplify customer interactions. As a result, the competitive landscape of IUL is increasingly being defined by those who best leverage tech-driven efficiencies.

The rise of robo-advisors is another trend enhancing the IUL landscape. These automated platforms use algorithms to provide financial advice and manage investment portfolios. By incorporating robo-advisory services, IUL insurers can offer real-time, data-driven investment strategies to their clients, often at a lower cost than traditional advisors. This democratization of financial advice makes IUL policies accessible to a broader audience, attracting younger generations who are savvy with technology and interested in digital-first financial solutions.

In conclusion, the incorporation of advanced technologies is ushering in a new era for Indexed Universal Life insurance. These innovations are enhancing the flexibility, transparency, and user-friendliness of IUL policies, making them more appealing and accessible to modern consumers. As technological advancements continue to evolve, we can expect to see further enhancements that will redefine the capabilities and reach of IUL, solidifying its position as a premier wealth-building tool in the digital age. Insurers who embrace these innovations will undoubtedly lead the charge in meeting the evolving demands of policyholders, securing a competitive advantage in an ever-changing marketplace.

Innovations in IUL Policy Design and Features

As we navigate the evolving landscape of Indexed Universal Life (IUL) insurance, it is imperative to examine the innovations that are redefining policy design and features. With advancements in technology, changing consumer demands, and an ever-fluctuating financial environment, IULs have experienced significant developments aimed at enhancing policyholder experience, maximizing growth potential, and providing superior adaptability. These innovations are transforming IULs from traditional insurance products into dynamic financial instruments that are increasingly capable of offering unparalleled wealth-building potential.

One of the notable innovations in IUL policy design is the expanded range of indexing options. Traditionally, IULs have primarily linked their cash value growth to broad market indexes like the S&P 500. However, insurance carriers are now introducing more diversified indexing strategies, including international indexes, hybrid indexes, and custom index options that combine several financial metrics. This diversification allows policyholders to tailor their IULs more closely to their individual risk tolerance and market outlook, potentially enhancing growth opportunities while managing downside risk more effectively.

Moreover, the design of cap rates, participation rates, and interest crediting strategies has become more sophisticated and dynamic. Insurers are now offering flexible cap rates that adjust in response to market conditions, providing policyholders with the potential for higher upside participation during strong market periods. Similarly, enhancements in participation rates have enabled policyholders to gain a greater percentage of index growth. Additionally, some insurers are integrating innovative crediting methods, such as the use of multiple index segments, which allocates cash value across different timelines and indexes to minimize volatility and optimize returns.

Another area where IUL policy design has evolved is in the realm of policy loan structures. Traditional IUL policies offered fixed and variable loan interest rates, which sometimes limited flexibility for policyholders seeking to access their cash value. However, the introduction of indexed loan options has revolutionized this aspect. Indexed loans enable policyholders to borrow against their policy while still participating in index growth, an attractive feature for those who wish to maintain wealth-building momentum even as they leverage their policy for liquidity.

Furthermore, new features are being introduced to enhance the longevity and sustainability of IUL policies. One such innovation is the addition of over loan protection riders, which prevent a policy from lapsing due to excessive borrowing. These riders ensure that policyholders can continue to benefit from their IULs without the risk of losing coverage, thus extending the utility of the policy over a lifetime.

Advanced policy management tools have also emerged as a significant trend. Insurers are utilizing cutting-edge digital platforms to enhance policyholder engagement and management. With user-friendly interfaces, policyholders can now track their cash value performance, simulate borrowing scenarios, and adjust premium allocations online. This digital accessibility not only empowers policyholders to make informed, strategic decisions but also reflects a broader trend of innovation across the financial services industry.

The incorporation of wellness programs and living benefits is yet another promising development in IUL policy design. Recognizing the growing emphasis on holistic financial well-being, some IUL policies now offer premium credits or additional bonuses for policyholders who engage in healthy lifestyle behaviors or participate in wellness programs. Additionally, living benefits such as long-term care or chronic illness riders are becoming standard features, providing valuable protection against life's uncertainties while preserving wealth-building opportunities.

As we consider these innovations, it becomes clear that the evolution of IUL policy design is driven by a desire to offer customers a comprehensive financial tool that adapts to their changing needs. The integration of diverse indexing strategies, adaptive pricing models, flexible loan options, and value-added features collectively enhance the appeal of IULs as a versatile wealth-building instrument. Moving forward, IUL policies are poised to become even more integrated with technology and personalized to user needs, contributing to their growth as a cornerstone of financial and estate planning strategy.

In conclusion, the innovative evolution in IUL policy design and features is not only enhancing the value proposition of these insurance products but also shaping the future of personal finance. As these trends continue to develop, IULs are set to offer even greater flexibility, control, and potential for policyholders, anchoring their reputation as a resilient and adaptive solution in the complex financial landscape.

Influence of Regulatory Changes on the IUL Market

The landscape of Indexed Universal Life (IUL) insurance has undergone significant shifts, largely influenced by evolving regulatory standards. As a dynamic financial tool, the IUL market is particularly susceptible to changes in regulatory frameworks, which can shape the extent of its viability and attractiveness as a wealth-building vehicle. In this section, we will explore how regulatory changes have historically impacted IUL policies, examine recent shifts, and discuss potential future regulatory trends that could influence the market.

Historical Context and Regulatory Foundations

To appreciate the current and future regulatory influences on the IUL market, it is essential to understand the foundational regulations that have governed life insurance and annuity products in the United States. The primary regulatory authority originates from state insurance departments, which have traditionally overseen the life insurance industry. This decentralized regulatory framework allows for variations in how IUL policies are marketed and sold across different states.

Historically, the introduction of the National Association of Insurance Commissioners' (NAIC) model regulations has played a crucial role in standardizing certain aspects of life insurance policy design and sales practices. By providing a model regulation for state insurance departments to adopt, the NAIC has contributed to creating a more cohesive regulatory environment for IUL products.

A significant milestone in the regulatory history of IUL was the adoption of Actuarial Guideline 49 (AG 49) in 2015. AG 49 was designed to address concerns about overly aggressive index crediting illustrations that could mislead policyholders regarding potential returns. By limiting the illustrated rates that insurers could use to project growth, AG 49 aimed to enhance transparency and protect consumers from unrealistic expectations.

Recent Regulatory Shifts

In response to the ongoing evolution of life insurance products and market conditions, the NAIC has continued to refine regulatory guidelines. A notable development was the subsequent introduction of AG 49-A in 2020, which further tightened restrictions on illustrated rates and imposed additional requirements on index-linked variable loans. This moves underscored regulators' commitment to ensuring fair practices and promoting consumer confidence in IUL offerings.

The regulatory emphasis on consumer protection has also led to heightened scrutiny of sales practices, particularly the marketing of IUL policies to seniors and vulnerable populations. Insurance regulators have increasingly prioritized initiatives to prevent misrepresentation and ensure that prospective policyholders fully understand the features and risks associated with IUL products.

Moreover, with the growing integration of digital tools in financial services, regulators have been exploring ways to adapt oversight mechanisms to encompass issues like cybersecurity and data privacy. This emphasis on digital regulation could influence the way IUL products are designed, marketed, and serviced, potentially affecting consumer access and operational efficiencies in the industry.

Anticipated Future Regulatory Trends

Looking ahead, the future of IUL regulation is poised to intersect with broader shifts in regulatory philosophy and policy-making priorities. One such trend is the increasing alignment with Environmental, Social, and Governance (ESG) criteria. As policymakers and the public place greater emphasis on sustainability and ethical business practices, life insurers, including those offering IUL policies, may experience regulatory nudges toward more transparent ESG reporting and alignment with climate-related financial disclosure standards.

Another anticipated regulatory evolution is the integration of technology and innovation in underwriting and policy administration. Insurtech advancements are propelling change in how life insurance products are priced and delivered. Regulators may soon institute guidelines to oversee automated underwriting processes, ensuring equitable access and preventing discrimination based on data analytics and algorithms.

There is also the possibility of regulatory shifts emanating from legislative action at the federal level. While life insurance regulation primarily resides with the states, pressures for federal oversight could arise, particularly concerning large, nationally operating insurers or when issues of national economic significance, like systemic risk, come into play.

In conclusion, the influence of regulatory changes on the IUL market is multifaceted and constantly evolving. While the core intent of regulation remains the protection of policyholders and the stability of the financial system, the specific mechanisms and focus of regulatory bodies will continue to shape the direction of the IUL industry. Stakeholders in the IUL space—insurers, agents, and policyholders alike—must remain vigilant, adapting to regulatory developments to leverage IUL policies effectively as a tool for tax-advantaged wealth building.

Predictive Analysis: Future Paths of IUL as a Wealth Tool

As we cast our gaze toward the financial landscape of tomorrow, Indexed Universal Life (IUL) insurance stands at a fascinating crossroads. It is no longer just an insurance product; it has metamorphosed into a sophisticated wealth-building tool that offers both protection and growth. This subpoint explores the future paths of IUL as a wealth instrument, leveraging its unique characteristics to seize emerging opportunities and navigate potential challenges in an increasingly complex economic world.

The Evolution of IUL as a Wealth Tool

Historically, life insurance products have been associated primarily with death benefits—safeguards against the uncertainties of life. However, the IUL policy, with its dynamic blend of life insurance and investment-like features, has redefined this space. It introduces an innovative mechanism where policyholders can allocate their cash value to track the performance of market indexes, such as the S&P 500. This evolution is set to persist, with even greater integration of sophisticated financial models aiming to maximize both growth potential and safety for policyholders.

Harnessing Technological Innovations

Looking forward, technology will be a linchpin in shaping the efficacy and appeal of IUL policies. The inclusion of advanced data analytics and artificial intelligence will enhance the ability to predict market trends and customer behavior, enabling more personalized product offerings that align closely with individual financial goals. Virtual financial advisors, powered by AI, could soon provide policyholders with real-time dashboards that visualize policy performance, predict future growth figures, and suggest optimized strategies tailored to personal circumstances.

Moreover, blockchain technology is poised to revolutionize transparency and efficiency within the insurance sector. Imagine an IUL platform where every policy detail is securely available and verifiable in real-time. This level of transparency will instill greater trust and accessibility, mitigating concerns over policy fees and performance track records.

Diversification and Customization

As IUL policies evolve, they will likely offer broader diversification options, enabling policyholders to allocate cash values across various indexes and asset classes. This diversification meets the growing demand for financial products that can withstand market volatility and economic downturn. In addition, customizable policy features will likely become more prevalent, allowing clients to tailor their policies not only to meet death-benefit needs but also to align with specific life stages and financial objectives, such as retirement planning or funding for education.

Debt strategies within IUL policies, particularly policy loans, will continue to gain traction. Leveraging the policy cash value to access liquidity without triggering tax events undeniably enhances its allure as a tax-efficient wealth management tool. Innovations in how these loans are structured, perhaps even with variable rate options tied to economic indicators, will further deepen the value proposition for sophisticated investors.

Regulatory Landscape and Its Implications

Regulation will play a crucial role in shaping the future paths of IUL as a wealth tool. Given its dual nature as both an insurance product and an investment vehicle, regulatory oversight will likely intensify. Policymakers will focus on ensuring transparency, fair representation, and the protection of consumers from potential misrepresentation of the product's capabilities and limitations.

However, regulatory changes could also open new avenues for developing more robust and flexible IUL structures. Any increased scrutiny may drive innovation, pushing insurers to develop more novel, compliant product designs that adhere to guidelines while maximizing consumer benefits.

Embracing Global Opportunities

As financial globalization intensifies, the prospect of cross-border offerings of IUL policies may become viable. The appetite for U.S.-based financial products is substantial within international markets, where investors seek reliable methods of preserving and growing wealth amidst economic and political uncertainties. By tailoring IUL offerings to meet the regulatory and cultural needs of different regions, insurers can tap into a vast pool of potential policyholders around the world.

A Holistic Financial Planning Tool

In the future, IUL is destined to solidify its role as not merely a standalone wealth-building tool but as an integral component of holistic financial planning. Advisors will increasingly incorporate IUL strategies alongside traditional vehicles like 401(k)s and IRAs, promoting its use as part of diversified financial portfolios aimed at hedging risk and enhancing tax efficiency.

As we journey through the 21st century, the confluence of innovation, customization, and proactive regulation will unlock an unprecedented paradigm, establishing IUL as a cornerstone of modern financial strategy. Those who leverage IUL's evolving capabilities stand to benefit richly from its promise.

Strategic Planning for Future IUL Policyholders and Investors

As the financial landscape continues to evolve, the role of Indexed Universal Life (IUL) insurance in strategic financial planning is poised to become even more significant. For those considering IUL as a component of their financial toolkit, strategic planning is pivotal, ensuring that policyholders and investors leverage the full spectrum of benefits that IUL policies offer. With thoughtful planning and proactive management, future IUL policyholders can unlock unique opportunities for wealth accumulation, tax efficiency, and financial security.

In approaching strategic planning, prospective IUL policyholders must first deepen their understanding of the intricate elements that make these policies unique. IUL is not a one-size-fits-all solution; rather, its benefits can be customized to meet individual financial goals. A key initial step is conducting a comprehensive needs analysis. This involves evaluating personal financial objectives, risk tolerance, and time horizons. Are you seeking to provide a tax-free death benefit for heirs? Is your primary goal long-term cash value accumulation with the potential for eventual tax-free withdrawals? Understanding your priorities sets the stage for tailoring an IUL policy to meet those specific criteria.

Once clear about the financial goals, the next crucial aspect is selecting the appropriate market index options that align with your risk appetite and financial objectives. With index selections such as the S&P 500 or the NASDAQ, policyholders can strategically allocate the cash value of their IUL to mirror their expectations of market performance. While the upside potential is attractive, it is equally important to be mindful of the policy's cap rates and participation rates, which dictate how much of the index gains are credited to the policy. Choosing indexes with historical resilience may offer more consistent returns over time.

Strategic planning must also account for premium funding strategies. IUL policies are distinct in their flexibility, allowing for variable premium payments. Strategically funding the policy with substantial premiums early on can maximize the compounding benefits of the cash value growth. However, overfunding must be balanced carefully to avoid the policy becoming a Modified Endowment Contract (MEC), which could result in unfavorable tax consequences. Thus, future policyholders should consider engaging with financial advisors to carefully project premium funding scenarios that align with both current cash flow capabilities and long-term objectives.

Tax efficiency remains one of IUL's standout features. As financial regulations and tax laws evolve, strategic planning will necessitate staying informed about potential legislative changes that could impact the benefits of IUL policies. Regularly reviewing the policy and making adjustments in response to these changes can help maintain the policy's tax-advantaged status. Additionally, strategic withdrawals and policy loans, executed correctly, can provide tax-free income during retirement—a benefit that requires understanding the nuances of policy minimums, maximum loan rates, and the timing of loans to avoid potential pitfalls such as policy lapses.

For investors considering IUL as part of a diversified portfolio, it is vital to recognize how IUL can complement other investment vehicles. With market volatility becoming a regular feature of the investment landscape, IUL's downside protection is a key strategic benefit. During market downturns, the guarantee that cash value will not decrease ensures that this element of the financial plan serves as a stabilizing force. Furthermore, the built-in life insurance benefit adds an additional layer of security, offering peace of mind that is often not present in traditional investment accounts.

Additionally, an often-underutilized aspect of strategic planning with IUL is its role in business financial strategies. Entrepreneurs and business owners can leverage IUL policies for business continuity planning, such as keyman insurance or funding buy-sell agreements. The implications of such strategic utilization extend beyond individual wealth-building to encompass fostering business resilience and succession planning.

In conclusion, strategic planning is an indispensable component for both future IUL policyholders and investors. This involves not just the initial selection of a suitable policy but an ongoing, dynamic assessment of financial goals, market conditions, and regulatory environments. By approaching IUL with a strategic mindset, individuals and business owners alike can harness the full breadth of opportunities these versatile financial tools offer. Achieving a deep understanding of IUL mechanics, customizing policy elements to meet future needs, and continually revisiting and adjusting strategies in response to an ever-changing landscape will ensure IUL remains a cornerstone of successful wealth-building strategies well into the future.

Chapter 12: The Future of Innovative IUL

Analysis of Current Market Trends in IUL

In the rapidly evolving landscape of financial products, Indexed Universal Life (IUL) insurance has fashioned its niche as a hybrid tool balancing life insurance with growth potential tied to market indexes. The current behaviors and preferences observed among IUL policyholders and insurers reflect a multifaceted interplay of economic, demographic, and psychological factors that continuously reshape this market.

One of the prominent trends currently seen in the IUL market is the widespread appeal of its dual benefit model — providing both a death benefit and a cash value component that can appreciate over time. This is particularly attractive in an era of financial uncertainty characterized by fluctuating economic conditions. As low-interest rates persist alongside volatile equity markets, many investors find solace in the stability and potential of IUL policies. They offer a harmonious blend of risk management through guaranteed minimum returns, and opportunity, leveraging the upside potential of market index-linked growth.

The last decade has exposed the vulnerabilities of traditional savings and investment vehicles, prompting a shift in consumer behavior. IULs are being increasingly positioned as a viable alternative. The global pandemic has further underscored the need for robust financial planning — with many individuals reassessing their risk tolerance and overall financial strategies. Unlike direct equity investments, IUL offers a safeguarded platform for growth with protective caps and reliable floors, thereby mitigating large losses during unfavorable market periods. This mechanism has resonated well with policyholders, especially those nearing retirement, who are looking to hedge against the depletion of savings during downturns.

Demographic shifts, naturally, exert a significant influence on the IUL market. An aging population, for instance, has heightened demand for products that offer lifelong financial security and estate planning benefits. Baby boomers, concerned about outliving their retirement funds, see IUL policies as a means to secure a continuous stream of tax-free income. In contrast, younger generations like Millennials and Gen Z, motivated by experiences of financial crises witnessed in their formative years, are more cognizant of the benefits of early financial planning. This demographic's increasing inclination towards IULs is fueled by the desire to create a safety net while simultaneously exploring growth opportunities.

Meanwhile, changing employment patterns also contribute to the evolving landscape of IUL demands. The gig economy has redefined traditional employment, with more individuals becoming freelancers and independent contractors. This new wave of workers, who often lack employer-provided benefits like retirement savings plans and life insurance, find IUL policies appealing for providing self-directed financial security. This trend underscores the adaptability of IUL in catering to diverse economic realities, supporting financial independence in unyielding times.

Another force driving momentum within the IUL market is the growing sophistication of consumers and their increased understanding of financial products. With access to information at their fingertips, today's policyholders are more inquisitive and value centric. They seek not just peace of mind but also transparency and adaptability in their investments. Insurers, in response, have become more innovative, refining IUL products with consumer-friendly features and customizable options to attract these discerning clients. This evolution has cultivated a market that prizes alignment with policyholder interests and ethical transparency.

Lastly, there is an undeniable rise in awareness regarding alternative investment strategies. Propelled by social media and digitization, financial literacy initiatives have enlightened consumers about the importance of diversifying one's financial portfolio. IUL's hybrid model stands as an attractive offshoot from traditional investment paths, appealing to those who exhibit an appetite for diversified exposure without relinquishing the foundational security offered by life insurance.

In conclusion, current market trends in the IUL space paint a compelling picture of a product witnessing increasing traction as a result of its alignment with contemporary economic and social dynamics. By thoughtfully catering to the modern policyholder's needs—be it through managing risks amidst fluctuating markets or addressing the financial concerns of an aging and employment-shifted demographic—IUL policies have positioned themselves not merely as insurance products, but as integral components of a comprehensive financial strategy. This is evidence of a promising trajectory that is likely to remain pivotal as the financial landscape continues to evolve in the coming years.

Technology and IUL: Driving Efficiency and Transparency

In recent years, the Indexed Universal Life (IUL) insurance landscape has been experiencing a transformative upheaval driven by rapid advancements in technology. As the financial services sector becomes increasingly digitized, the nexus between IUL policies and technology is poised to redefine the future of this financial product. Within this evolving environment, the advent of robo-advisors, artificial intelligence (AI)-driven analytics, and blockchain technology stands at the forefront, creating ripples across the IUL industry. Each of these technological innovations plays a pivotal role in ensuring that IUL policies are more efficient, transparent, secure, and appealing, particularly to the younger generations who are increasingly leaning towards tech-savvy financial tools.

Robo-advisors have emerged as a game-changer in the financial services industry, bringing with them a new era of automation and efficiency in managing investments, including IUL policies. These automated platforms leverage complex algorithms to automate administrative tasks, optimize the performance of IUL policies, and enhance client-user interaction. With robo-advisors, policyholders can receive hands-on, intuitive management of their IUL policies with minimal manual intervention. This not only minimizes human error but also allows for near real-time adjustments in investment strategies linked to the policy's cash value. Moreover, by reducing reliance on traditional advisory services, policyholders incur fewer advisory fees, making IUL products more cost-effective and accessible. Consequently, these automated platforms are making IUL policies more attractive to the tech-savvy millennial and Gen Z demographics who prioritize digital, user-friendly financial solutions.

Parallel to these advancements is the utilization of AI-driven analytics, which are revolutionizing the personalized management of IUL policies. AI technologies empower insurers to analyze vast amounts of data and extract valuable insights into policyholder preferences and behaviors. By integrating AI analytics, insurers can tailor IUL policy features to meet the unique needs and goals of individual clients. For instance, predictive analytics can be employed to anticipate market trends and policy performance, allowing policyholders to make informed decisions about premium allocations and cash value growth strategies. Additionally, AI-driven tools can customize communication strategies between insurers and policyholders, ensuring personalized interactions that enhance customer satisfaction and engagement. Essentially, AI is transforming the personalization aspect of IUL policies, making them more aligned with individual financial aspirations and risk tolerances.

Blockchain technology, often synonymous with transparency and security, is another cornerstone in the technological overhaul of IUL policies. The decentralized nature of blockchain creates an immutable, transparent ledger system that enhances the reliability and security of policy transactions. By incorporating blockchain, insurers can guarantee the authenticity and accuracy of policy records, reducing the risk of fraud and errors. This level of transparency builds trust between policyholders and insurers, which is crucial in an industry so reliant on long-term relationships. Additionally, blockchain facilitates streamlined reporting and auditing processes, further enhancing efficiency in policy management. Financial consumers, especially the younger generation, value security and transparency in their financial dealings, and blockchain fulfills these demands, thus broadening the appeal of IUL policies to a wider audience.

These technological advances are not only reshaping how IUL policies are managed but also making them more appealing to a younger, tech-savvy demographic that demands innovation and efficiency in their financial tools. The integration of user-friendly digital interfaces and advanced data analytics in IUL management aligns with the expectations of a generation that values convenience, customization, and transparency. Thus, the tech-driven evolution of the IUL landscape stands as a compelling testament to the commitment of the insurance industry to evolving with the times, all while remaining rooted in providing secure, adaptable wealth-building solutions.

In conclusion, as these technological innovations continue to permeate into the fabric of IUL policies, they promise to create a more dynamic and resilient insurance product. The harnessing of robo-advisors, AI, and blockchain is not merely an enhancement of current practices but a reinvention of the IUL experience — one that is poised to meet the needs of the modern consumer. As the industry continues to embrace these tools, the potential for Indexed Universal Life insurance to maintain its place as a premier wealth-building instrument is both promising and certain.

Innovations in IUL Policy Design

In the rapidly evolving world of financial products, Indexed Universal Life (IUL) insurance stands out due to its unique blend of life insurance protection and investment potential. As insurers strive to keep pace with changing market demands and consumer preferences, they have made significant strides in innovating IUL policy design. These innovations cater to a wide range of financial goals and risk appetites, positioning IUL policies as indispensable tools in modern financial planning.

One of the most notable advancements in IUL policy design is the introduction of multi-index options. Traditionally, IUL policies were linked to a single index, such as the S&P 500. While this provided a solid foundation for potential cash value growth, it limited policyholders to the performance of one particular market indicator. The introduction of multi-index strategies has transformed this landscape by allowing policyholders to diversify their exposure across multiple indexes, such as the NASDAQ-100, Dow Jones, or even international indexes like the Euro Stoxx 50. This diversification not only offers broader growth opportunities but also helps mitigate risk by spreading investments across various sectors and economic regions.

Another crucial innovation in the IUL market is the flexibility to switch indexes on an annual basis. This feature provides policyholders with an adaptive strategy to respond to changing economic climates and personal financial objectives. By allowing annual index switching, insurers empower their clients to take advantage of favorable market conditions or to avoid downturns in specific sectors. This flexibility is particularly appealing for those who seek active participation in their financial planning and who wish to align their life insurance policies more closely with their broader investment strategies.

Incorporating partial downside protection features is yet another groundbreaking development in IUL policy design. Traditionally, one of the keys selling points of an IUL was its built-in protection of principal against market losses—if the index linked to the policy performed poorly, the credited interest rate would simply be zero, thus safeguarding the policy's cash value. However, innovations have elevated this concept by introducing partial downside protection options. These features allow policyholders to customize their level of risk tolerance more precisely. For instance, some modern IUL policies offer the option to choose a buffered index account, where the insurer absorbs a predetermined percentage of market loss. This can be particularly advantageous for more risk-averse consumers who are willing to sacrifice a portion of potential upside gains to ensure greater stability in turbulent markets.

Insurers are also pioneering ways to address specific financial goals through more tailored IUL products. For example, some policies now offer advanced riders and options that cater to diverse objectives such as retirement income, college funding, or even specific estate planning needs. The ability to add features like a long-term care rider or a chronic illness rider further enhances the policy's utility as a comprehensive financial planning tool. These additions allow policyholders to customize their coverage and benefits better, aligning their insurance policies with their overall financial and life goals.

Moreover, the integration of digital tools and platforms in IUL policy management has improved both accessibility and user experience. Insurers are increasingly providing online portals and mobile applications to allow policyholders to track the performance of their chosen indexes, adjust allocations, and manage account details with unprecedented ease. This technological integration not only makes managing IUL policies more convenient but also enhances consumer engagement by providing real-time insights and data-driven decision-making tools.

The cumulative effect of these innovations is the creation of an increasingly attractive and versatile IUL product. As these policies become more flexible and tailored to individual needs, they are predicted to gain wider acceptance among a broader demographic, transcending traditional market segments. By addressing diverse consumer financial goals and risk appetites, insurers are positioning IULs as vital components of holistic wealth management strategies. This evolution signifies not just a trend but a transformation in how life insurance can be leveraged as a dynamic financial planning resource, underscoring its potential as a future-forward wealth-building tool.

In conclusion, the innovations in IUL policy design exemplify the insurance industry's responsiveness to changing consumer demands and economic conditions. As these policies become more adaptable and sophisticated, they offer exciting new possibilities for individuals seeking to protect their financial futures while capturing growth opportunities. This evolution bears testament to the industry's commitment to innovation, aiming to transform IULs into indispensable assets in the landscape of personal finance and wealth management.

Emerging Challenges and Regulatory Influences

As the Indexed Universal Life (IUL) insurance market continues its expansion, it is not immune to potential challenges that could impede its growth trajectory. Among the most significant factors are regulatory changes, economic downturns, and fluctuations in interest rates. Each of these elements can influence how IUL products are designed, structured, and perceived by consumers, making them critical considerations for industry stakeholders.

Regulatory Challenges

The regulatory landscape is one of the most significant factors affecting the evolution of IUL products. Regulatory bodies, such as the National Association of Insurance Commissioners (NAIC) and state insurance departments, play an essential role in overseeing how IUL policies operate. These entities ensure consumer protection and the financial soundness of insurance companies. As the IUL market matures, regulators tend to scrutinize the assumptions made in illustrations, transparency in policy features, and how products are marketed to consumers.

Recent regulatory changes reflect an increased focus on ensuring that policy illustrations provide a realistic outlook on performance, amidst concerns that some representations might have been overly optimistic. For instance, regulators have been closely examining the cap rate—the maximum rate of return that a policyholder can earn in any given period based on the performance of underlying market indexes—and the participation rate, which determines how much of the index's gain is credited to the insurance policy.

Additionally, the introduction of new guidelines, such as Actuarial Guideline 49 (AG 49) and its subsequent updates, targets the presentation of index-linked products and aims to make them more consistent and consumer-friendly. Such regulations impact the way insurers calculate and disclose policy benefits, potentially affecting the overall appeal of IULs. As regulators continue to prioritize transparency and consumer protection, insurers might be required to recalibrate how these policies are structured and presented, possibly introducing design adjustments that align with updated compliance standards.

Economic Challenges

Economic downturns pose a substantial threat to the IUL market, primarily because these products are intertwined with capital markets. A sluggish economy can lead to lower consumer confidence and reduced discretionary spending, impacting on the demand for financial products like IUL.

Moreover, the performance of IUL policies is closely linked to market indexes. Therefore, during economic downturns, when these indexes often underperform, both existing policyholders and potential buyers might view IULs as less attractive due to diminished returns. Consequently, insurers may need to reassess their strategies for managing policyholder expectations and enhancing policy features that can safeguard against adverse economic conditions.

Interest Rate Fluctuations

Interest rate environments significantly affect the dynamics of IULs. Historically low interest rates have been a double-edged sword. On one hand, they have bolstered the appeal of IULs as the search for higher yields drove consumers toward alternative investment vehicles. On the other hand, low rates can compress margins for insurers, affecting their ability to offer attractive cap and participation rates.

If interest rates rise, there can be pressures on the mechanics of IUL products. Insurers might be able to offer better cap rates due to higher expected returns from their underlying investment portfolios. However, this scenario could also steer consumers towards more traditional fixed-income products, thereby challenging IULs' relative appeal.

In light of such interest rate fluctuations, insurance companies are tasked with the challenge of maintaining policy competitiveness while ensuring profitability. They may respond by innovating policy designs or adjusting pricing structures to remain attractive compared to other financial instruments.

Proactive Industry Strategies

In response to these multi-faceted challenges, the industry has been proactive in employing innovative strategies to mitigate risks and seize opportunities. Insurers are increasingly focusing on product diversification and adopting advanced risk management techniques to fortify their IUL offerings against external pressures.

In conclusion, while the IUL market is poised for continued growth, its trajectory is closely tied to regulatory, economic, and interest rate conditions. Insurers, regulators, and consumers must stay vigilant and adaptive to navigate these dynamic challenges successfully. Through regulatory compliance, innovative product design, and transparent communication, the IUL market can sustain its position as a valuable tool for wealth building in a complex financial landscape.

Predictions for IUL as a Wealth-Building Tool

As we peer into the future of financial planning, Indexed Universal Life (IUL) insurance policies are poised to become an increasingly vital component of personal and family wealth-building strategies. The current economic environment, with its often-volatile financial markets, low interest rates, and a growing emphasis on securing tax-advantaged financial vehicles, provides a ripe backdrop for the evolution and broader adoption of IUL policies as a cornerstone of prudent financial stewardship.

At the heart of this prediction lies the fundamental capability of IUL to offer a unique blend of death benefit protection and market-linked growth potential, coupled with principal protection. This combination continues to be appealing against the backdrop of an investment landscape characterized by uncertainty and heightened market risks. As more individuals seek stable yet rewarding growth paths without the direct exposure to market volatility, the built-in safety net of IUL's floor guarantees is likely to attract a wider audience, thereby cementing its role as a preferred wealth-building tool.

Looking forward, it's reasonable to predict that IUL policies will evolve to include even more sophisticated features, catering to diversified financial goals and personal preferences.

Insurers are likely to innovate by incorporating a broader array of index options beyond traditional benchmarks like the S&P 500. These could include indices that capture emerging markets, technology sectors, or even ESG (Environmental, Social, and Governance) priorities, providing policyholders with tailor-made vehicles that align with their values and financial objectives.

Further, the need for flexibility in financial planning will drive enhancements in the design of IUL policies. We may see the advent of more modular policy structures that allow for dynamic adjustments in premium payments, face amounts, and index selections. Such adaptability will be crucial in accommodating the life changes and unpredictable financial needs of policyholders, from young professionals looking to balance debt repayment and savings, to retirees seeking to maximize retirement income without outliving their resources.

Consumer attitudes towards insurance and savings are also likely to undergo significant shifts. As financial literacy becomes more prevalent, particularly among younger generations, there will be a growing recognition of the benefits of integrating insurance and investment. Therefore, IUL policies, with their dual offering of wealth protection and growth, will increasingly be perceived as a prudent means of achieving financial security across life stages. This trend could result in earlier policy adoption, with younger policyholders investing into IULs as foundational elements of their financial portfolios rather than as late-stage acquisitions for wealth transfer or estate planning.

Moreover, the tax advantages provided by IULs—such as tax-deferred cash value growth and tax-free loans—will become even more attractive as fiscal policies evolve. Should changes in tax legislation occur that heighten the burden on capital gains or traditional retirement vehicles, the relative appeal of using IUL policies as a tax-optimized approach for wealth accumulation and legacy planning is likely to soar.

Addressing the increasing complexity and interconnectedness of the global financial landscape, the future of IUL policies may also see technological integrations that provide greater transparency and control for policyholders. Insurtech advancements, including AI-driven analytics and personalized dashboards, could empower policyholders to monitor performance, simulate strategies, and make informed decisions with real-time data, thus enhancing the overall client experience and satisfaction.

Lastly, the role of IUL in legacy planning is expected to expand as consumers become more proactive in securing multigenerational wealth transfer. The ability to lock in a tax-free death benefit assures the preservation of family wealth and the perpetuation of financial success and stability for future generations. In this context, advisors and insurers will need to provide enhanced guidance and tools that facilitate seamless integration of IUL policies with broader estate strategies.

In conclusion, IUL policies are set to play an increasingly pivotal role in the wealth-building matrices for individuals and families. As the financial world grapples with evolving challenges and opportunities, IUL offers a versatile and robust solution that adapts to both anticipated and unforeseen changes. By marrying protection with growth potential, offering tax-efficient avenues, and enabling flexible policy management, IUL stands ready to meet the dynamic needs of contemporary financial planning, securing its place as a cornerstone of future wealth-building strategies.

Integration of IUL within Broader Financial Strategies

In the ever-evolving landscape of financial planning, the seamless integration of Indexed Universal Life (IUL) insurance with other financial strategies holds immense potential. As individuals increasingly seek robust, diversified portfolios to safeguard and enhance their wealth, IUL emerges as a versatile financial tool that can harmonize effectively with traditional retirement instruments like 401(k)s, IRAs, and real estate investments. This integration not only supports long-term financial health but also enriches legacy planning, offering a comprehensive approach to wealth management.

Synergies Between IUL and Retirement Planning Tools

One of the most compelling aspects of IUL is its ability to offer tax-advantaged growth and distribution. Unlike traditional retirement accounts such as 401(k)s and IRAs, which are often subject to hefty tax implications upon withdrawal, IUL provides the added benefit of tax-deferred growth and potentially tax-free loans. This characteristic allows IUL to act as a powerful supplement to other retirement accounts, offering liquidity and flexibility that can effectively bridge income gaps during retirement.

For instance, during periods of market downturns, retirees might refrain from tapping into their 401(k) or IRA to avoid selling assets at a loss. IUL policies, with their cash value component, offer an alternative source of funds during such times. The cash value can be accessed through policy loans, often tax-free, if the policy is properly structured, thereby preserving the other retirement accounts for growth during recovery periods.

Furthermore, IUL can provide a safety net that addresses the distribution phase's tax implications. By integrating IUL into a broader retirement strategy, individuals might optimize their tax liabilities, balancing withdrawals across different accounts to maintain a lower tax bracket. This strategic distribution becomes increasingly crucial as retirees aim to preserve their savings over longer lifespans.

IUL and Real Estate Investments

Real estate, with its potential for appreciation and passive income, remains a cornerstone of many investment portfolios. However, it is not without its risks and liquidity challenges. Here, IUL plays a pivotal role in risk management and liquidity provision. The cash value of an IUL can offer liquidity to cover unexpected property expenses, mitigate vacancy periods, or finance additional real estate acquisitions without the immediate need for liquidating real estate assets.

Moreover, since the cash value in IULs can grow based on indexed interest credits linked to market performance (without direct market risks), it can balance the cyclical nature of real estate investments. This synergy provides a more stable platform for long-term financial growth.

The Role of Professional Financial Planners

As the financial landscape becomes increasingly complex, the role of professional financial planners is paramount in navigating these intricacies. Financial planners are particularly crucial in the successful integration of IUL within broader, diversified portfolios. They possess the expertise to tailor IUL policies according to client-specific financial goals, risk tolerance, and estate planning needs, ensuring that the client's entire financial picture is both coherent and optimized for maximum benefit.

Financial planners help individuals construct a coherent strategy where IUL is not just a standalone product but a component within a fully diversified portfolio. This means seamlessly blending IUL with stocks, bonds, real estate, and other retirement vehicles, taking into account factors like tax implications, risk management, and income needs.

In addition, planners are instrumental in educating clients about the nuances of IUL, including its benefits and limitations. This understanding enables clients to make informed decisions and leverage IUL policies to their fullest potential, aligning them with both immediate and future financial objectives.

Future Prospects of IUL in Financial Planning

Looking ahead, the integration of IUL within broader financial strategies is set to flourish. As clients seek to enhance financial resilience and maximize legacy potential, IUL in combination with traditional investment vehicles will become increasingly appealing. Innovations in policy design, increased client education, and enhanced financial technologies will facilitate more seamless integration and contribute to a broader acceptance and utilization of IUL in comprehensive financial planning.

In conclusion, as part of an integrated financial strategy, IUL offers unique advantages that align with both wealth accumulation and protection. By working synergistically with other financial tools, IUL enhances flexibility, tax efficiency, and risk management, playing a pivotal role in securing financial futures and building lasting legacies. Ultimately, the expert guidance of financial planners will be essential in harnessing the full potential of IUL within this broader context, enabling individuals to navigate their financial journeys with confidence and precision.

About the Author

STACIE GASTON

Stacie Gaston is a respected voice in the world of personal finance, known for making complex financial concepts accessible, actionable, and empowering. With a background in wealth strategy and a strong passion for financial literacy, she has helped countless individuals navigate the path to financial independence using innovative tools like Indexed Universal Life Insurance (IUL).

Over the years, Stacie has dedicated her career to uncovering the strategies the wealthy use to grow and protect their assets—and showing everyday people how to do the same. Her approach blends proven principles with modern techniques to help readers build tax-free retirement income, protect their families, and create generational wealth.

In this book, Stacie shares her insights with clarity and candor, offering readers a practical roadmap to a more secure and prosperous future.

When she's not writing or advising, Stacie enjoys traveling, mentoring aspiring entrepreneurs, and spending time with her family. She believes financial freedom is not just a destination—but a lifestyle that begins with knowledge and intentional action.

"Financial empowerment doesn't belong to the elite—it belongs to anyone willing to learn the rules of the game and play it smart."
— Stacie Gaston

Made in the USA
Middletown, DE
02 June 2025